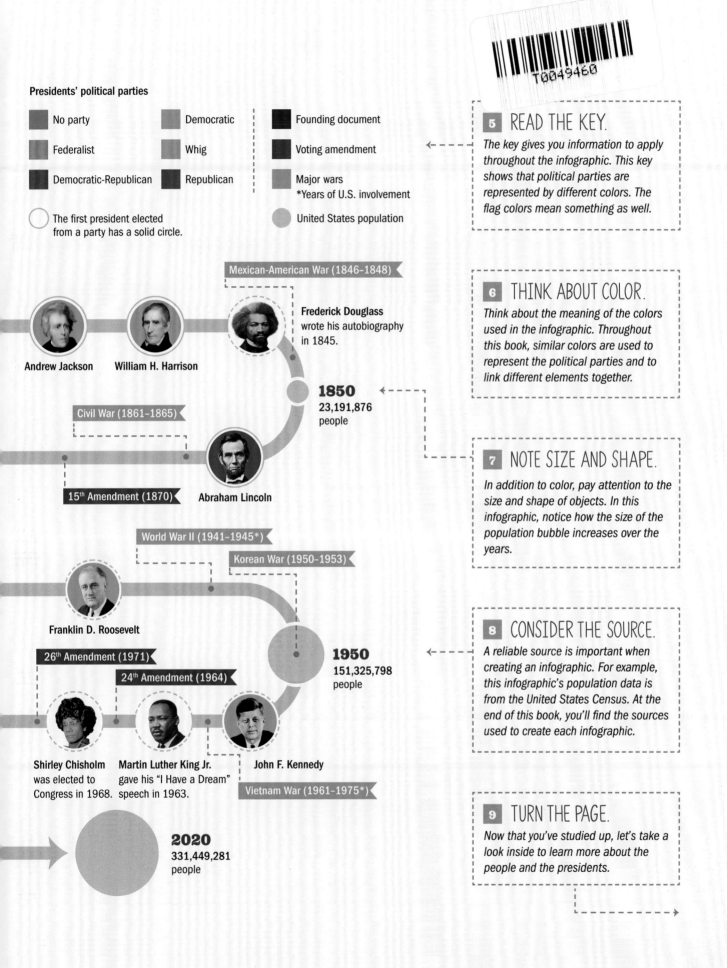

Presidents' political parties

- No party
- Federalist
- Democratic-Republican
- Democratic
- Whig
- Republican

- Founding document
- Voting amendment
- Major wars
  *Years of U.S. involvement
- United States population

The first president elected from a party has a solid circle.

Mexican-American War (1846–1848)

Andrew Jackson   William H. Harrison

Frederick Douglass wrote his autobiography in 1845.

Civil War (1861–1865)

1850
23,191,876
people

15th Amendment (1870)   Abraham Lincoln

World War II (1941–1945*)

Korean War (1950–1953)

Franklin D. Roosevelt

26th Amendment (1971)

24th Amendment (1964)

1950
151,325,798
people

Shirley Chisholm was elected to Congress in 1968.

Martin Luther King Jr. gave his "I Have a Dream" speech in 1963.

John F. Kennedy

Vietnam War (1961–1975*)

2020
331,449,281
people

5 READ THE KEY.

The key gives you information to apply throughout the infographic. This key shows that political parties are represented by different colors. The flag colors mean something as well.

6 THINK ABOUT COLOR.

Think about the meaning of the colors used in the infographic. Throughout this book, similar colors are used to represent the political parties and to link different elements together.

7 NOTE SIZE AND SHAPE.

In addition to color, pay attention to the size and shape of objects. In this infographic, notice how the size of the population bubble increases over the years.

8 CONSIDER THE SOURCE.

A reliable source is important when creating an infographic. For example, this infographic's population data is from the United States Census. At the end of this book, you'll find the sources used to create each infographic.

9 TURN THE PAGE.

Now that you've studied up, let's take a look inside to learn more about the people and the presidents.

T0049460

To our children,
Noah, Everett, and Charlotte

Published by Roaring Brook Press

Roaring Brook Press is a division of Holtzbrinck Publishing Holdings Limited Partnership

120 Broadway, New York, NY 10271 · mackids.com

ISBN 978-1-62672-469-3

Library of Congress Control Number 2021906533

Our books may be purchased in bulk for promotional, educational, or business use.

Please contact your local bookseller or the Macmillan Corporate and Premium Sales Department at

(800) 221-7945 ext. 5442 or by email at MacmillanSpecialMarkets@macmillan.com.

First edition, 2021 · Book design by Mike Burroughs

PJ Creek used Adobe Illustrator to create the infographics in this book.

Printed in China by RR Donnelley Asia Printing Solutions Ltd., Dongguan City, Guangdong Province

1 3 5 7 9 10 8 6 4 2

PERIODICPRESIDENTS.COM

WE THE PEOPLE AND THE PRESIDENT

An Infographic Look at the American Presidency

PJ CREEK *AND* **JAMIE CREEK**

Roaring Brook Press · New York

Power to the People

Throughout history, people have been ruled by kings, queens, pharaohs, emperors, and dictators. These systems put power in the hands of one person. Our democratic system, based on the Constitution, places power in the hands of the people. Today's world governments are not always clear-cut, as some fit into more than one category.

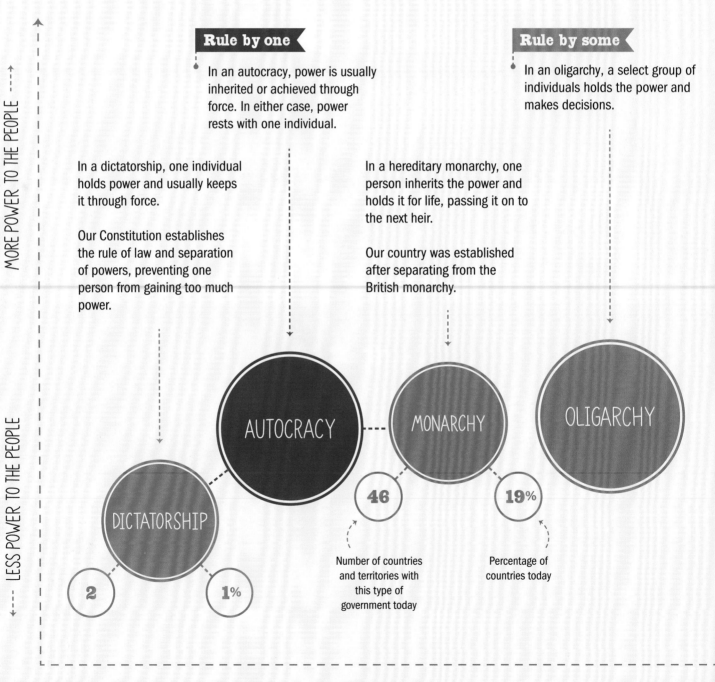

Rule by one

In an autocracy, power is usually inherited or achieved through force. In either case, power rests with one individual.

In a dictatorship, one individual holds power and usually keeps it through force.

Our Constitution establishes the rule of law and separation of powers, preventing one person from gaining too much power.

In a hereditary monarchy, one person inherits the power and holds it for life, passing it on to the next heir.

Our country was established after separating from the British monarchy.

Rule by some

In an oligarchy, a select group of individuals holds the power and makes decisions.

MORE POWER TO THE PEOPLE

LESS POWER TO THE PEOPLE

DICTATORSHIP

AUTOCRACY

MONARCHY

OLIGARCHY

2

1%

46

Number of countries and territories with this type of government today

19%

Percentage of countries today

TYPE OF GOVERNMENT

This bubble is off the chart. Anarchy means no government or rule of law, so the people have all the power.

We tend to think power in the hands of the people is a good thing, but is this too much? In the world today, we often see anarchy during transitions of power.

ANARCHY

Rule by many

In a democracy, the people hold the power.

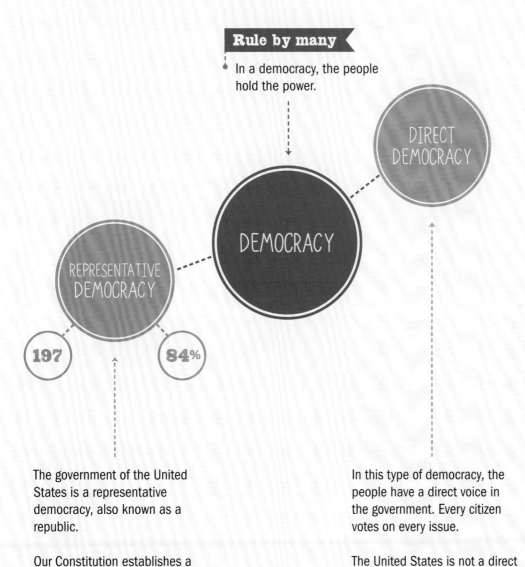

DIRECT DEMOCRACY

DEMOCRACY

REPRESENTATIVE DEMOCRACY

197   84%

The government of the United States is a representative democracy, also known as a republic.

Our Constitution establishes a system in which the people elect officials to represent them in the government.

In this type of democracy, the people have a direct voice in the government. Every citizen votes on every issue.

The United States is not a direct democracy. In a country our size, this type of government isn't practical.

In our democracy, you have power. The more you learn about our government system, the more power you have to shape it.

From the first three words of the Constitution, the architects of this government placed the power in the hands of the people. As a blueprint for our government, the Constitution is based on the rule of law. We are ruled by rules, not rulers. We the people have changed over the years, but the power we hold has remained the same. Let's explore our nation's founding document by the numbers.

3,929,214

PEOPLE

The first census, in 1790, counted almost 4 million Americans. This number included enslaved people, but did not include the many Native American nations.

THE OLDEST

SEPTEMBER 17,

1787

On this date, the Constitution was signed at the Constitutional Convention in Philadelphia, Pennsylvania.

OVER

230

YEARS OLD

Our Constitution has been around for a while. In fact, it's the oldest written national constitution used in the world today.

7,502

WORDS

Our entire national government is set up in some seven thousand words. Even with the twenty-seven amendments, the Constitution is relatively brief.

4

PAGES

The Constitution is stored at the National Archives in Washington, D.C. It's enclosed in argon-filled cases with titanium frames.

0

TIMES

Notably, the words *democracy* and *education* don't appear in the text. Political parties are not mentioned either.

3/5

OF A PERSON

As originally stated in the Constitution, people who were enslaved were not citizens and were counted as three-fifths of a person in congressional representation.

12%

OF THE POPULATION

After the Constitution was adopted, it's estimated that only 12% of the American population could vote in elections.

331,449,281

AMERICANS

Today, the Constitution is the foundation for a government that serves hundreds of millions of Americans.

18

YEARS OLD

Today, nearly all citizens 18 years of age and older are eligible to vote in elections. Some states place voting restrictions on convicted felons.

27

AMENDMENTS

The genius of the Constitution is that it can be changed through the amendment process. We've made twenty-seven changes so far.

People

26-81

YEARS OLD

All men, all white, all pretty wealthy, the signers ranged in age from 26 (Jonathan Dayton) to 81 (Benjamin Franklin).

2

PRESIDENTS

On the last page of the Constitution, after Article VII, you'll find the signatures of two future presidents: George Washington and James Madison.

7

ARTICLES

The Constitution is made of only seven articles. Turn the page to see where the president fits in.

THE CONTENTS

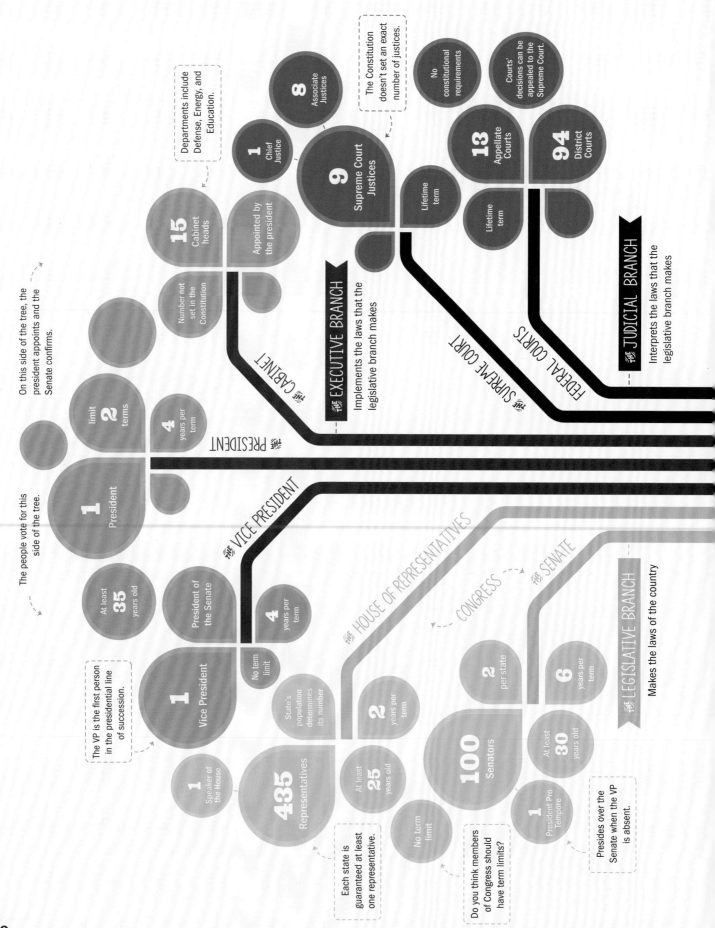

The people vote for this side of the tree.

On this side of the tree, the president appoints and the Senate confirms.

Departments include Defense, Energy, and Education.

The Constitution doesn't set an exact number of justices.

No constitutional requirements

Courts' decisions can be appealed to the Supreme Court.

8 Associate Justices

1 Chief Justice

9 Supreme Court Justices

13 Appellate Courts

94 District Courts

Lifetime term

Lifetime term

15 Cabinet heads

Appointed by the president

Number not set in the Constitution

THE CABINET

THE EXECUTIVE BRANCH
Implements the laws that the legislative branch makes

THE SUPREME COURT

FEDERAL COURTS

THE JUDICIAL BRANCH
Interprets the laws that the legislative branch makes

limit **2** terms

4 years per term

1 President

THE PRESIDENT

At least **35** years old

VICE PRESIDENT

The VP is the first person in the presidential line of succession.

President of the Senate

No term limit

4 years per term

1 Vice President

State's population determines its number

HOUSE OF REPRESENTATIVES

CONGRESS

THE SENATE

LEGISLATIVE BRANCH
Makes the laws of the country

2 per state

6 years per term

2 years per term

100 Senators

At least **30** years old

1 Speaker of the House

435 Representatives

At least **25** years old

No term limit

1 President Pro Tempore

Each state is guaranteed at least one representative.

Do you think members of Congress should have term limits?

Presides over the Senate when the VP is absent.

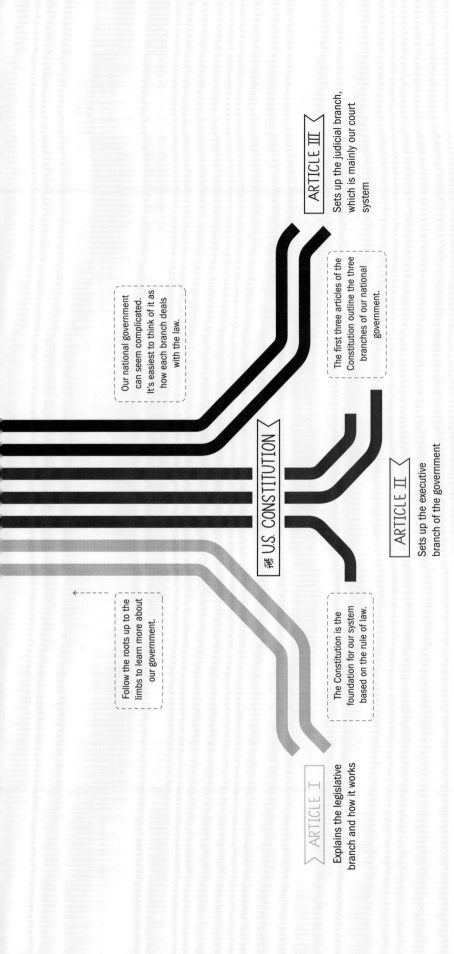

Our national government can seem complicated. It's easiest to think of it as how each branch deals with the law.

The first three articles of the Constitution outline the three branches of our national government.

ARTICLE III

Sets up the judicial branch, which is mainly our court system

U.S. CONSTITUTION

ARTICLE II

Sets up the executive branch of the government

Follow the roots up to the limbs to learn more about our government.

The Constitution is the foundation for our system based on the rule of law.

ARTICLE I

Explains the legislative branch and how it works

THE Government Tree

Our national government has been standing strong for centuries. It has weathered changing political climates, numerous election seasons, and even a civil war. Rooted in the Constitution, the national government is divided into three branches, each with separate and distinct powers. We the people are the caretakers of this government. It is our participation that keeps it healthy.

THE Periodic Table OF THE Presidents

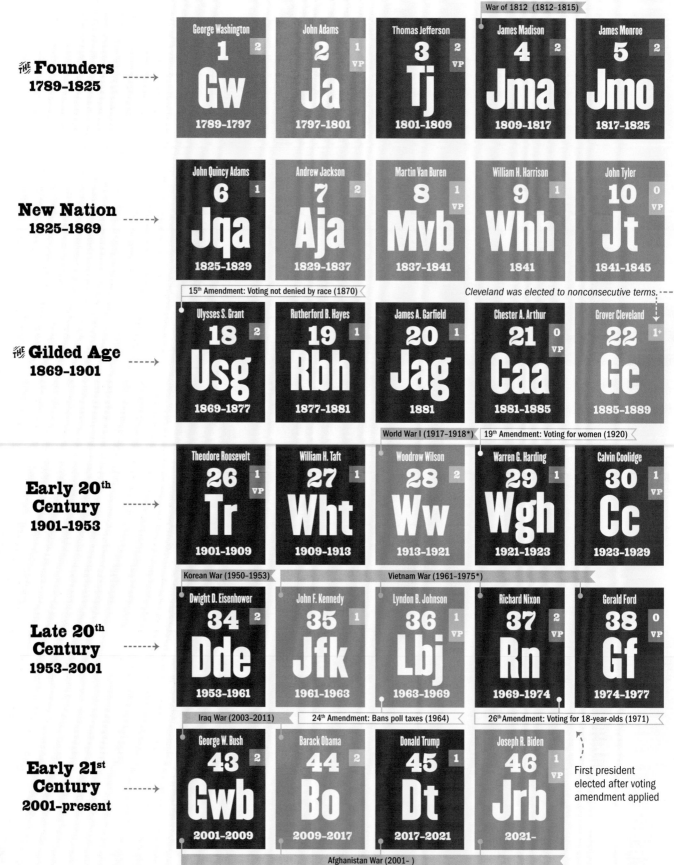

THE Founders
1789–1825

New Nation
1825–1869

THE Gilded Age
1869–1901

Early 20th Century
1901–1953

Late 20th Century
1953–2001

Early 21st Century
2001–present

War of 1812 (1812–1815)

George Washington	John Adams	Thomas Jefferson	James Madison	James Monroe
1 — 2	2 — 1 VP	3 — 2 VP	4 — 2	5 — 2
Gw	**Ja**	**Tj**	**Jma**	**Jmo**
1789–1797	1797–1801	1801–1809	1809–1817	1817–1825

John Quincy Adams	Andrew Jackson	Martin Van Buren	William H. Harrison	John Tyler
6 — 1	7 — 2	8 — 1 VP	9 — 1	10 — 0 VP
Jqa	**Aja**	**Mvb**	**Whh**	**Jt**
1825–1829	1829–1837	1837–1841	1841	1841–1845

15th Amendment: Voting not denied by race (1870)

Cleveland was elected to nonconsecutive terms.

Ulysses S. Grant	Rutherford B. Hayes	James A. Garfield	Chester A. Arthur	Grover Cleveland
18 — 2	19 — 1	20 — 1	21 — 0 VP	22 — 1+
Usg	**Rbh**	**Jag**	**Caa**	**Gc**
1869–1877	1877–1881	1881	1881–1885	1885–1889

World War I (1917–1918*) | 19th Amendment: Voting for women (1920)

Theodore Roosevelt	William H. Taft	Woodrow Wilson	Warren G. Harding	Calvin Coolidge
26 — 1 VP	27 — 1	28 — 2	29 — 1	30 — 1 VP
Tr	**Wht**	**Ww**	**Wgh**	**Cc**
1901–1909	1909–1913	1913–1921	1921–1923	1923–1929

Korean War (1950–1953) | Vietnam War (1961–1975*)

Dwight D. Eisenhower	John F. Kennedy	Lyndon B. Johnson	Richard Nixon	Gerald Ford
34 — 2	35 — 1	36 — 1 VP	37 — 2 VP	38 — 0 VP
Dde	**Jfk**	**Lbj**	**Rn**	**Gf**
1953–1961	1961–1963	1963–1969	1969–1974	1974–1977

Iraq War (2003–2011) | 24th Amendment: Bans poll taxes (1964) | 26th Amendment: Voting for 18-year-olds (1971)

George W. Bush	Barack Obama	Donald Trump	Joseph R. Biden
43 — 2	44 — 2	45 — 1	46 — 1 VP
Gwb	**Bo**	**Dt**	**Jrb**
2001–2009	2009–2017	2017–2021	2021–

First president elected after voting amendment applied

Afghanistan War (2001–)

Forty-five men have served as president so far (Grover Cleveland was both the 22nd and the 24th president). Political parties and historical periods bond them together. The great ones possess properties of a solid leader and leave a positive, lasting impact on the presidency. The not-so-great presidents may have been too reactive or didn't rise to the occasion. All have served the country as its chief executive.

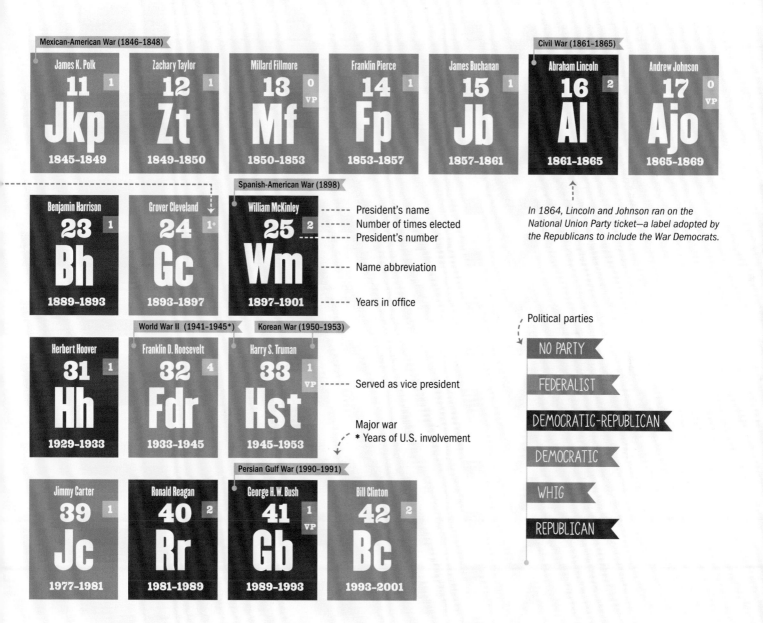

Mexican-American War (1846–1848)

Civil War (1861–1865)

James K. Polk	Zachary Taylor	Millard Fillmore	Franklin Pierce	James Buchanan	Abraham Lincoln	Andrew Johnson
11 1	**12** 1	**13** 0 VP	**14** 1	**15** 1	**16** 2	**17** 0 VP
Jkp	**Zt**	**Mf**	**Fp**	**Jb**	**Al**	**Ajo**
1845–1849	1849–1850	1850–1853	1853–1857	1857–1861	1861–1865	1865–1869

Spanish-American War (1898)

Benjamin Harrison	Grover Cleveland	William McKinley
23 1	**24** 1+	**25** 2
Bh	**Gc**	**Wm**
1889–1893	1893–1897	1897–1901

- - - - - President's name
- - - - - Number of times elected
- - - - - President's number

- - - - - - Name abbreviation

- - - - - - Years in office

In 1864, Lincoln and Johnson ran on the National Union Party ticket—a label adopted by the Republicans to include the War Democrats.

World War II (1941–1945*) — Korean War (1950–1953)

Herbert Hoover	Franklin D. Roosevelt	Harry S. Truman
31 1	**32** 4	**33** 1 VP
Hh	**Fdr**	**Hst**
1929–1933	1933–1945	1945–1953

- - - - - - Served as vice president

Major war
* Years of U.S. involvement

Political parties

NO PARTY

FEDERALIST

DEMOCRATIC-REPUBLICAN

DEMOCRATIC

WHIG

REPUBLICAN

Persian Gulf War (1990–1991)

Jimmy Carter	Ronald Reagan	George H. W. Bush	Bill Clinton
39 1	**40** 2	**41** 1 VP	**42** 2
Jc	**Rr**	**Gb**	**Bc**
1977–1981	1981–1989	1989–1993	1993–2001

By THE Numbers

All forty-five presidents share at least three similarities—those required by the Constitution. Their other shared characteristics may reflect the times in which they served, for better or for worse. What a president has been is not always what a president will be.

12
generals

THE THREE REQUIREMENTS

1. A natural-born citizen of the United States
2. A resident for at least 14 years
3. At least 35 years old

17
state governors

31
served in the military

15
served as VP

GENERALLY SPEAKING
Although not a requirement, military experience has been key to Election Day success. Dwight D. Eisenhower was the last general to be elected president.

Bubble sizes are relative to this one.

45
Presidents

Remember: Cleveland counts as the 22nd and 24th presidents.

27
lawyers

DEFENDING THE CONSTITUTION
Whether practicing it or writing it, knowing the law benefits a president. Abraham Lincoln was a successful lawyer before becoming president.

26
served in Congress

33
with blue or gray eyes

BLUE EYES?
This unlikely similarity points to a lack of diversity in the White House. Franklin Pierce was known for his piercing gray eyes.

9
served in House only

1 Speaker of the House

10
served in House & Senate

7
served in Senate only

8
with brown or black eyes

4
with hazel eyes

1 President pro tempore

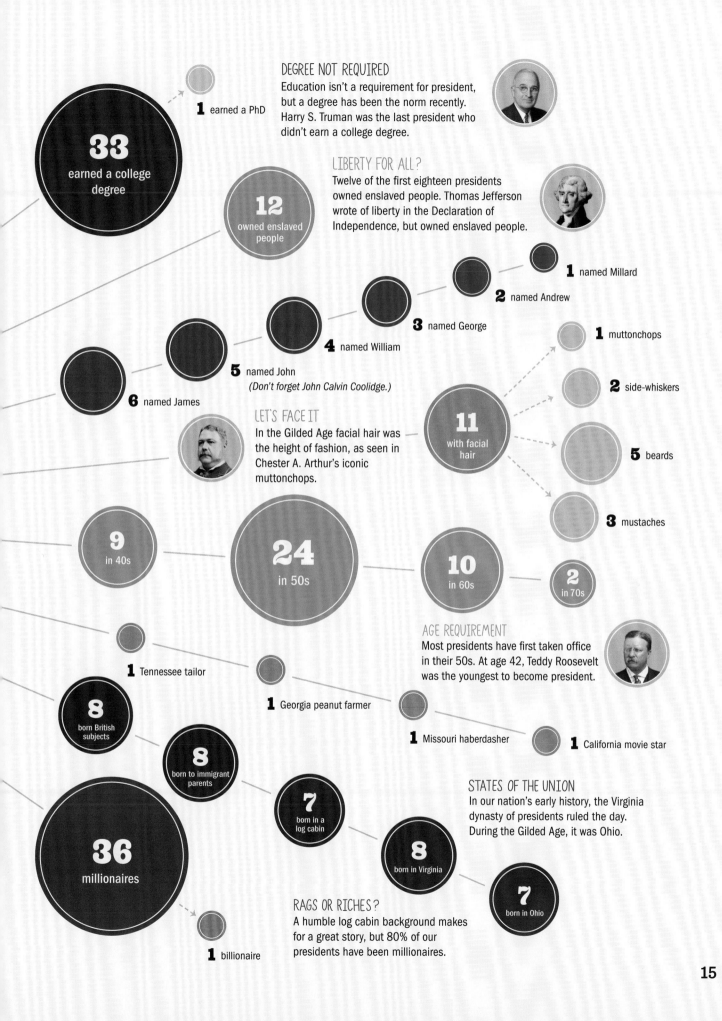

33 earned a college degree

1 earned a PhD

DEGREE NOT REQUIRED
Education isn't a requirement for president, but a degree has been the norm recently. Harry S. Truman was the last president who didn't earn a college degree.

LIBERTY FOR ALL?
Twelve of the first eighteen presidents owned enslaved people. Thomas Jefferson wrote of liberty in the Declaration of Independence, but owned enslaved people.

12 owned enslaved people

1 named Millard

2 named Andrew

3 named George

4 named William

5 named John
(Don't forget John Calvin Coolidge.)

6 named James

1 muttonchops

2 side-whiskers

5 beards

3 mustaches

11 with facial hair

LET'S FACE IT
In the Gilded Age facial hair was the height of fashion, as seen in Chester A. Arthur's iconic muttonchops.

9 in 40s

24 in 50s

10 in 60s

2 in 70s

AGE REQUIREMENT
Most presidents have first taken office in their 50s. At age 42, Teddy Roosevelt was the youngest to become president.

1 Tennessee tailor

1 Georgia peanut farmer

1 Missouri haberdasher

1 California movie star

8 born British subjects

8 born to immigrant parents

7 born in a log cabin

STATES OF THE UNION
In our nation's early history, the Virginia dynasty of presidents ruled the day. During the Gilded Age, it was Ohio.

8 born in Virginia

7 born in Ohio

36 millionaires

RAGS OR RICHES?
A humble log cabin background makes for a great story, but 80% of our presidents have been millionaires.

1 billionaire

15

Family Album

...ight we find in a president's family album? We may discover
...members who came to America from another country. Or we
...en find other presidents.

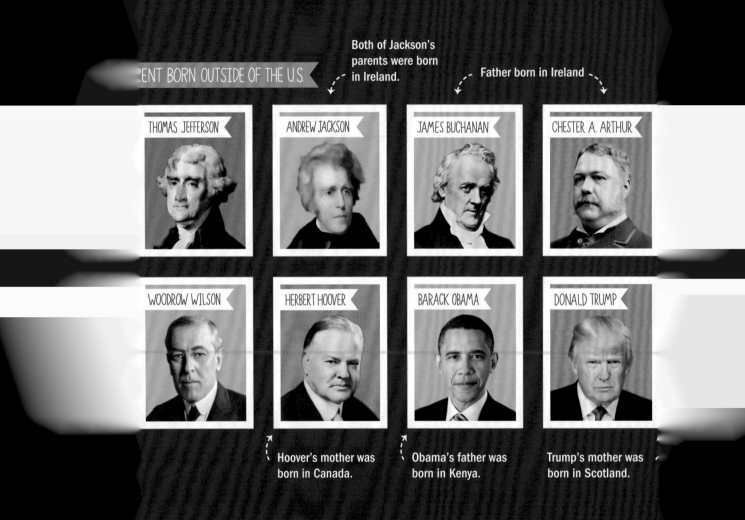

PRESIDENT BORN OUTSIDE OF THE U.S.

Both of Jackson's parents were born in Ireland.

Father born in Ireland

THOMAS JEFFERSON

ANDREW JACKSON

JAMES BUCHANAN

CHESTER A. ARTHUR

WOODROW WILSON

HERBERT HOOVER

BARACK OBAMA

DONALD TRUMP

Hoover's mother was born in Canada.

Obama's father was born in Kenya.

Trump's mother was born in Scotland.

FIRST BORN AS A U.S. CITIZEN

MARTIN VAN BUREN

The first seven presidents and William Henry
Harrison were born British subjects, as the
United States wasn't a country until after the
American Revolution.

Martin Van Buren was the first president
born as an American citizen.

JOHN ADAMS

JOHN QUINCY ADAMS

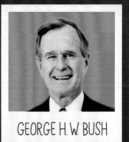

GEORGE H. W. BUSH

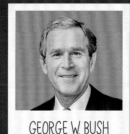

GEORGE W. BUSH

John Adams and John Quincy Adams were the first father-son duo to be elected president. Their family connection to the New World goes way back: John Adams's great-great-grandparents were Pilgrims.

John and John Quincy experienced similar careers: both went to Harvard, both were lawyers, and both were elected for only one term as president.

George H. W. Bush and George W. Bush were the second father-son duo to reach the White House.

Both Bushes went to Yale but followed different paths to the White House. George H. W. Bush was a pilot, congressman, CIA director, and VP. George W. Bush was in the National Guard, owned a baseball team, and served as governor of Texas.

GRANDFATHER-GRANDSON

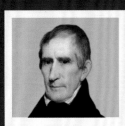

WILLIAM H. HARRISON

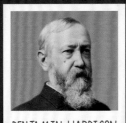

BENJAMIN HARRISON

The Harrison family goes back to the founding of the nation. Benjamin Harrison V signed the Declaration of Independence. His son, William Henry, became a war hero and president.

William Henry's grandson, Benjamin, continued the family legacy when he was elected president in 1888.

COUSINS

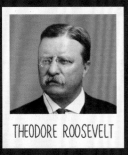

THEODORE ROOSEVELT

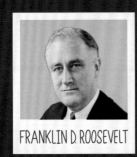

FRANKLIN D. ROOSEVELT

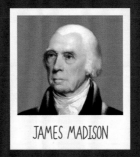

JAMES MADISON

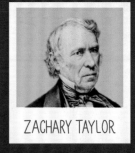

ZACHARY TAYLOR

The Roosevelts were fifth cousins. Teddy was the uncle of Eleanor Roosevelt. In fact, when Franklin and Eleanor married, Teddy gave the bride away.

James and Zachary were second cousins. The Father of the Constitution is related to the president who voted for the first time in his own election.

17

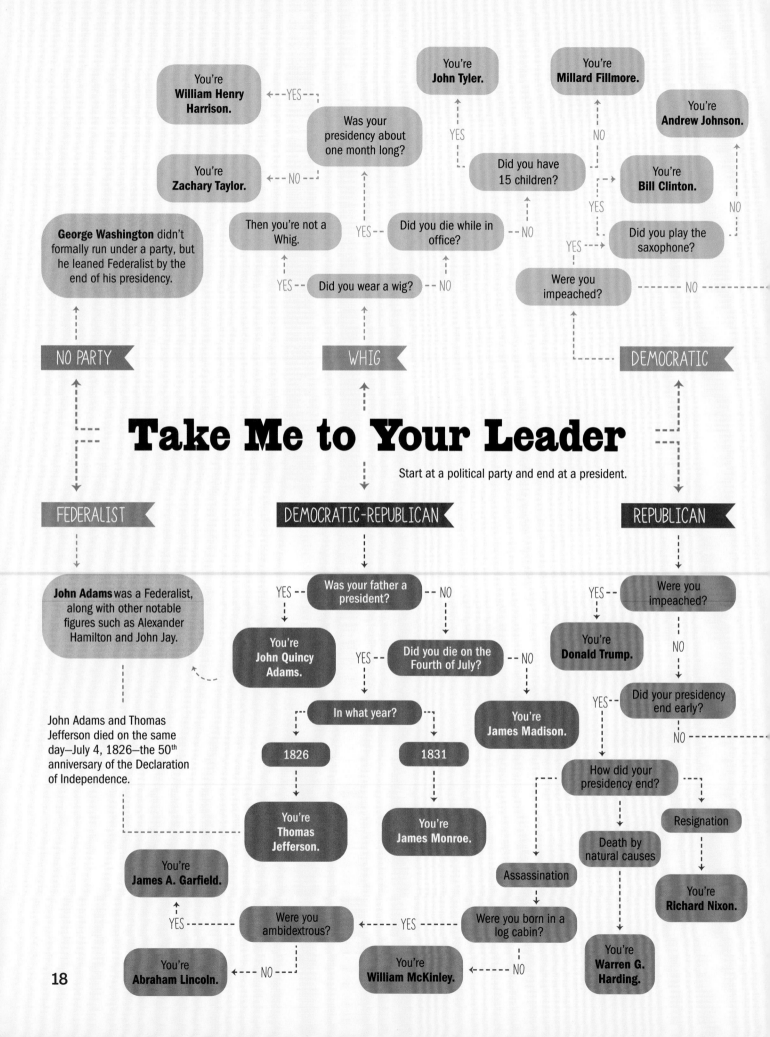

Take Me to Your Leader

Start at a political party and end at a president.

You're **William Henry Harrison.** ← -- YES -- ┐

You're **Zachary Taylor.** ← -- NO -- ┘

Was your presidency about one month long?

You're **John Tyler.**

YES

You're **Millard Fillmore.**

NO

You're **Andrew Johnson.**

You're **Bill Clinton.**

YES

Did you have 15 children?

NO

George Washington didn't formally run under a party, but he leaned Federalist by the end of his presidency.

Then you're not a Whig.

Did you die while in office? -- NO

YES

YES

Did you play the saxophone?

Did you wear a wig? -- NO

Were you impeached? ----- NO -----

NO PARTY

WHIG

DEMOCRATIC

FEDERALIST

DEMOCRATIC-REPUBLICAN

REPUBLICAN

John Adams was a Federalist, along with other notable figures such as Alexander Hamilton and John Jay.

John Adams and Thomas Jefferson died on the same day—July 4, 1826—the 50th anniversary of the Declaration of Independence.

YES -- Was your father a president? -- NO

You're **John Quincy Adams.**

YES -- Did you die on the Fourth of July? -- NO

You're **James Madison.**

Were you impeached?

YES --

You're **Donald Trump.**

NO

Did your presidency end early?

YES

NO

In what year?

1826

1831

You're **Thomas Jefferson.**

You're **James Monroe.**

How did your presidency end?

Resignation

Death by natural causes

You're **James A. Garfield.**

YES --- Were you ambidextrous? ← --- YES --- Were you born in a log cabin?

Assassination

You're **Richard Nixon.**

You're **Abraham Lincoln.** -- NO

You're **William McKinley.**

-- NO

You're **Warren G. Harding.**

18

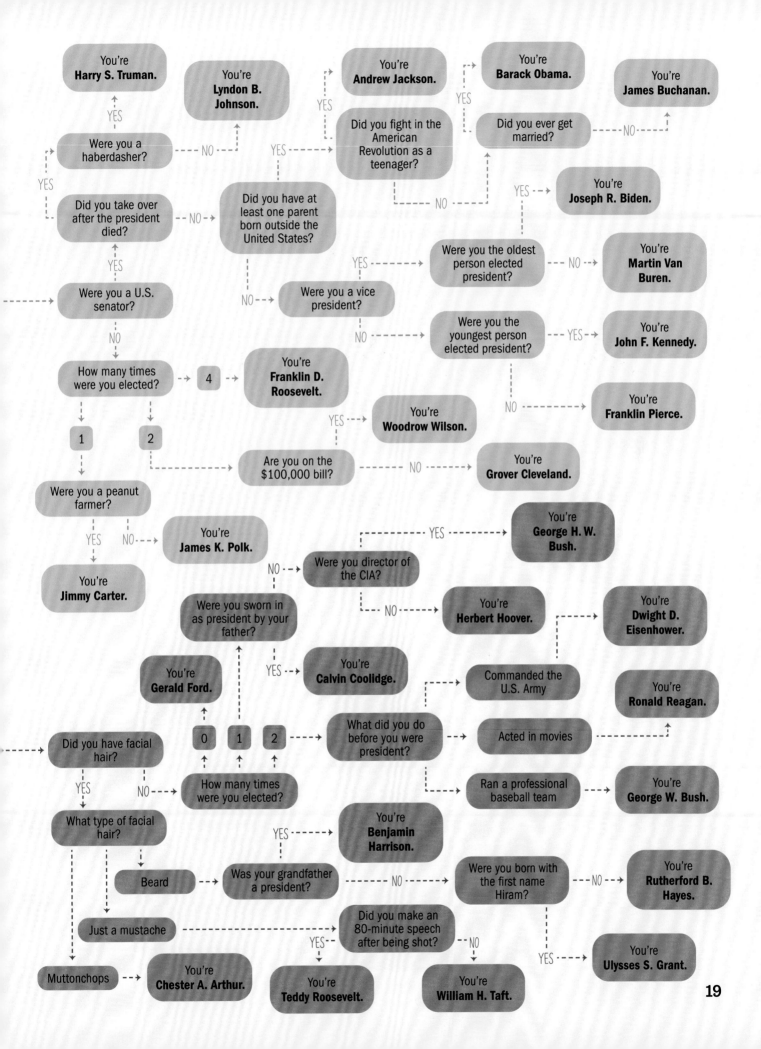

You're **Harry S. Truman.**

YES

Were you a haberdasher?

--- NO ---

YES

Did you take over after the president died?

--- NO ---

YES

Were you a U.S. senator?

NO

How many times were you elected?

→ 4 →

You're **Franklin D. Roosevelt.**

1   2

Were you a peanut farmer?

YES   NO ---→

You're **Jimmy Carter.**

You're **Lyndon B. Johnson.**

YES

Did you have at least one parent born outside the United States?

NO ---→

Were you a vice president?

YES

You're **Andrew Jackson.**

Did you fight in the American Revolution as a teenager?

NO

YES ---→

You're **Barack Obama.**

YES

Did you ever get married?

--- NO ---→

You're **James Buchanan.**

YES ---→

You're **Joseph R. Biden.**

Were you the oldest person elected president?

--- NO ---→

You're **Martin Van Buren.**

NO ---→

Were you the youngest person elected president?

--- YES ---→

You're **John F. Kennedy.**

NO

You're **Franklin Pierce.**

YES ---→

You're **Woodrow Wilson.**

Are you on the $100,000 bill?

--- NO ---→

You're **Grover Cleveland.**

You're **James K. Polk.**

--- YES ---→

You're **George H. W. Bush.**

NO --→

Were you director of the CIA?

--- NO ---→

You're **Herbert Hoover.**

You're **Dwight D. Eisenhower.**

Were you sworn in as president by your father?

YES ---→

You're **Calvin Coolidge.**

Commanded the U.S. Army

You're **Ronald Reagan.**

You're **Gerald Ford.**

0   1   2 →

What did you do before you were president?

--→

Acted in movies

Did you have facial hair?

YES   NO ---→

How many times were you elected?

Ran a professional baseball team

--→

You're **George W. Bush.**

What type of facial hair?

YES ---→

You're **Benjamin Harrison.**

Beard

--→

Was your grandfather a president?

--- NO ---→

Were you born with the first name Hiram?

--- NO --→

You're **Rutherford B. Hayes.**

Just a mustache

Did you make an 80-minute speech after being shot?

YES

NO

YES ---→

You're **Ulysses S. Grant.**

Muttonchops --→

You're **Chester A. Arthur.**

You're **Teddy Roosevelt.**

You're **William H. Taft.**

19

ᴛʜᴇ Political Parties Prism

Political parties emerged in the earliest days of our nation. Each party creates a platform that reflects its ideas. From taxes to social issues, the parties' platforms span a wide spectrum of ideas. Let's take a look at the founding principles of the parties that have won the White House.

▮ No party

Our first president didn't truly belong to any political party. In fact, in his farewell address, he warned of the danger of political parties. If anything, Washington leaned Federalist.

1789 ◀--- First election win

GEORGE WASHINGTON

▮ Federalist

Named for its support of a federal constitution, the Federalist Party focused on a strong central government and a society forged by industry and manufacturing.

1796 ◀

JOHN ADAMS

▮ Democratic-Republican

As the first opposition political party, the Democratic-Republicans believed in a small government, states' rights, and a society rooted in farming.

1800 ◀

THOMAS JEFFERSON

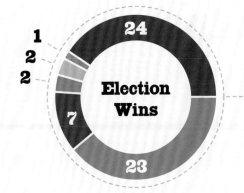

24

1
2
2

Election Wins

7

23

Over the years, the Republican Party has taken the lead on the presidential election scoreboard. The Democrats are close behind.

Democratic

The Democratic Party began as a faction of the Democratic-Republicans who supported Andrew Jackson. The party appealed to the "common man," who now had more say in choosing the president.

1828

ANDREW JACKSON

Whig

The Whig Party emerged in opposition to Andrew Jackson. Like the Federalists before them, the Whigs believed in a strong central government. The Whig Party also supported business and a national bank.

1840

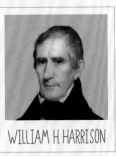

WILLIAM H. HARRISON

Republican

The Party of Lincoln began as a combination of Whigs, Free-Soilers, and Northern Democrats who stood against the expansion of slavery and supported industrial growth.

1860

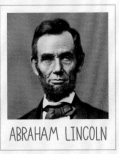

ABRAHAM LINCOLN

Along Party Lines

Political parties bounce to the left and right, often changing direction at major turning points. At each turn, the American voter has been offered two main choices. We call it the two-party system, and historians usually divide it into five eras. Since the 1850s, the two major party names have stayed the same, but their core ideas have changed.

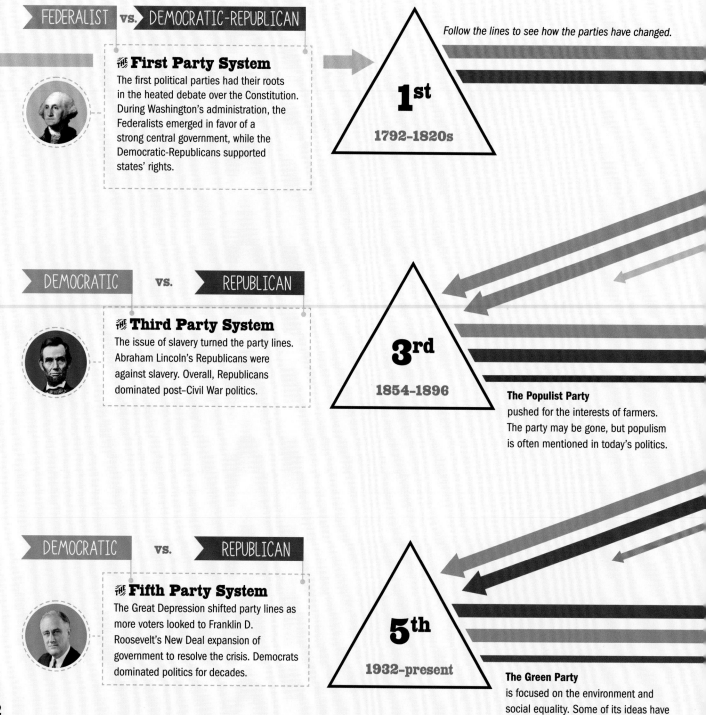

FEDERALIST **vs.** DEMOCRATIC-REPUBLICAN

Follow the lines to see how the parties have changed.

☞ First Party System
The first political parties had their roots in the heated debate over the Constitution. During Washington's administration, the Federalists emerged in favor of a strong central government, while the Democratic-Republicans supported states' rights.

1st
1792–1820s

DEMOCRATIC **vs.** REPUBLICAN

☞ Third Party System
The issue of slavery turned the party lines. Abraham Lincoln's Republicans were against slavery. Overall, Republicans dominated post–Civil War politics.

3rd
1854–1896

The Populist Party
pushed for the interests of farmers. The party may be gone, but populism is often mentioned in today's politics.

DEMOCRATIC **vs.** REPUBLICAN

☞ Fifth Party System
The Great Depression shifted party lines as more voters looked to Franklin D. Roosevelt's New Deal expansion of government to resolve the crisis. Democrats dominated politics for decades.

5th
1932–present

The Green Party
is focused on the environment and social equality. Some of its ideas have been adopted by the Democratic Party.

NOTABLE THIRD PARTIES

Free-Soil

Populist

Progressive

Green

Third parties usually emerge around a particular issue of their day. At times, their ideas are absorbed into a major party.

DEMOCRATIC vs. WHIG

Second Party System

Andrew Jackson's Democratic Party ushered in a new era, but the Whigs tried to end the reign of King Andrew. Jackson's Democrats barely resemble the party of today.

2nd
1828–1854

The Free-Soil Party
aimed to prevent slavery's expansion. Former president Martin Van Buren ran for the party in 1848.

DEMOCRATIC vs. REPUBLICAN

Fourth Party System

In the early 1900s, the Party of Lincoln turned its attention to business and industry. The Democratic Party found support in the "Solid South," but it wasn't enough. The Republicans dominated the White House again in this era.

4th
1896–1932

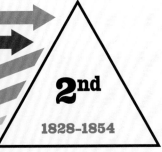

The Progressive Party
made a run in the early 1910s, demanding reforms in society and industry. Former president Teddy Roosevelt ran in 1912.

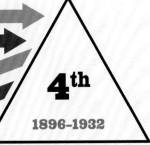

WHAT'S NEXT?

Sixth Party System?

It may be too soon to tell. Some historians say it started with the election of Richard Nixon and a shift toward more conservative politics. The question remains: How long will it continue to be a choice of red or blue?

Red State, Blue State

On Election Night, Americans everywhere watch as states across the nation turn red or blue. Popular votes are tallied, and the winner gains electoral votes. Some states offer big payoffs in the count. Others offer a small scorecard bump. In the end, the candidate who wins enough states to reach 270 wins the presidency. Let's take a closer look at the trends from the last four presidential elections.

270 electoral votes are needed to win—just over half of the total 538 electoral votes.

In the last four elections ----->

RED STATES

Voted Republican all four times

DO THE MATH

A state's electoral votes are calculated by adding its number of representatives (depends on population) and its number of senators (all states have two). Take Oregon, for example.

6 + **2** = **8**

Members in the House of Representatives

Members in the Senate

Electoral votes

WINNER TAKES ALL

In a red state, over half of the people voted for the Republican candidate, and in a blue state, over half of the people voted for the Democratic candidate.

In every state (except Maine and Nebraska), the winning candidate receives all of that state's electoral votes.

With 54 electoral votes, California has been the biggest blue prize in recent elections.

POPULATION, NOT AREA

At first glance, the map appears to have a lot more red than blue. But electoral votes depend on a state's population, not its land area. The small state of Hawaii has more electoral votes (4) than the large state of Alaska (3).

FOUR SCORES (AND SEVERAL YEARS AGO)

Check out the electoral vote totals from the last four elections. Then take a look at the map to see how each state voted.

In 2016, a handful of faithless electors cast votes for other candidates.

2008		2012		2016		2020	
OBAMA	365	OBAMA	332	TRUMP	304	BIDEN	306
McCAIN	173	ROMNEY	206	H.CLINTON	227	TRUMP	232

LIGHT RED STATES
Voted Republican three times and Democratic once

PURPLE STATES
Voted Democratic twice and Republican twice

LIGHT BLUE STATES
Voted Democratic three times and Republican once

BLUE STATES
Voted Democratic all four times

WINNER TAKES SOME

States decide how to allocate electoral votes. Maine and Nebraska don't have a winner-takes-all system. Instead, their votes are split by who wins each congressional district.

Can you imagine what the map would look like if every state had a system like that?

BATTLEGROUND STATES

Known by many names: battleground states, toss-up states, swing states. The outcomes in these states often determine the winner of an election.

AN OUTDATED SYSTEM?

Do you think the electoral system represents the American people, or do you think it should be changed?

With 40 electoral votes, Texas has been the biggest red prize in recent years.

Florida's 30 electoral votes make it the most valuable battleground state.

25

Counting the People

Every ten years, the U.S. government counts the American people with the Census. It's required by the Constitution and is used to determine representation in Congress. Over time, the Census has gathered a lot of information about America and its people.

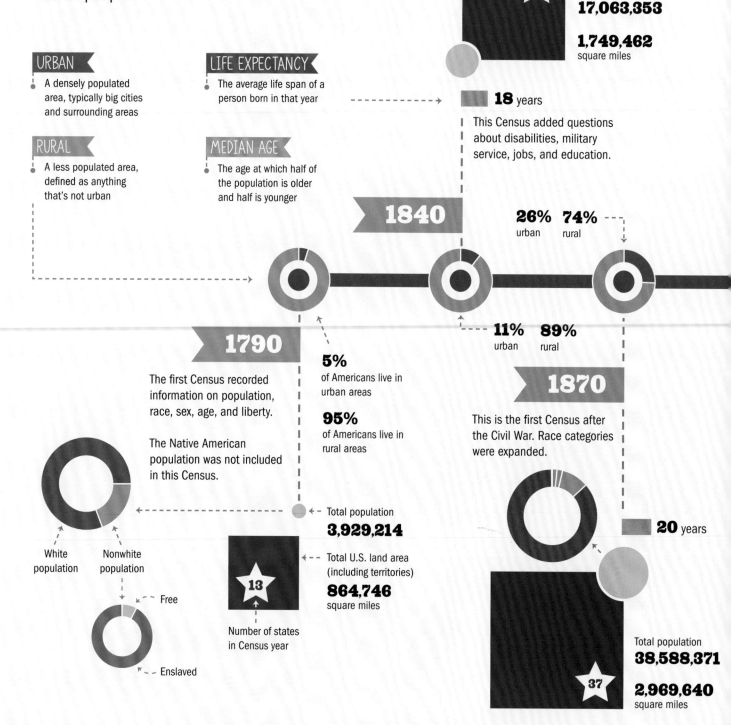

URBAN
A densely populated area, typically big cities and surrounding areas

RURAL
A less populated area, defined as anything that's not urban

LIFE EXPECTANCY
The average life span of a person born in that year

MEDIAN AGE
The age at which half of the population is older and half is younger

26
Total population
17,063,353

1,749,462
square miles

18 years

This Census added questions about disabilities, military service, jobs, and education.

1840

26% urban **74%** rural

11% urban **89%** rural

1790

The first Census recorded information on population, race, sex, age, and liberty.

The Native American population was not included in this Census.

5%
of Americans live in urban areas

95%
of Americans live in rural areas

White population   Nonwhite population

Free

Enslaved

13
Number of states in Census year

Total population
3,929,214

Total U.S. land area (including territories)
864,746
square miles

1870

This is the first Census after the Civil War. Race categories were expanded.

20 years

Total population
38,588,371

2,969,640
square miles

37

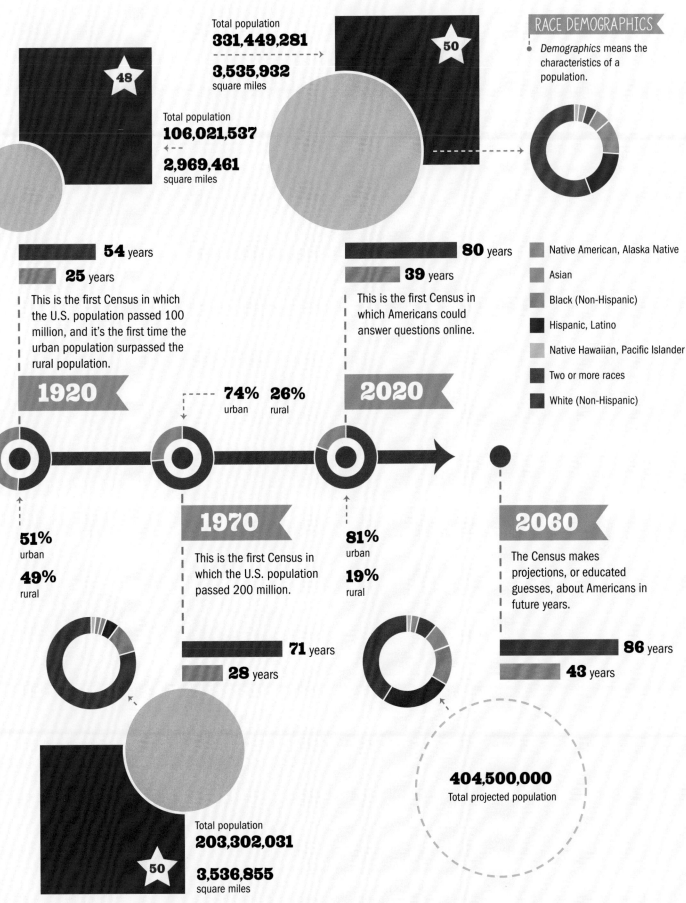

Total population
331,449,281

3,535,932
square miles

Total population
106,021,537

2,969,461
square miles

Demographics means the characteristics of a population.

54 years

25 years

This is the first Census in which the U.S. population passed 100 million, and it's the first time the urban population surpassed the rural population.

1920

80 years

39 years

This is the first Census in which Americans could answer questions online.

Native American, Alaska Native

Asian

Black (Non-Hispanic)

Hispanic, Latino

Native Hawaiian, Pacific Islander

Two or more races

White (Non-Hispanic)

74% urban **26%** rural

2020

51%
urban

49%
rural

1970

This is the first Census in which the U.S. population passed 200 million.

81%
urban

19%
rural

2060

The Census makes projections, or educated guesses, about Americans in future years.

71 years

28 years

86 years

43 years

Total population
203,302,031

3,536,855
square miles

404,500,000
Total projected population

27

THE Issues That Divide Us

As Americans, we are united as citizens of the same country. However, certain issues tend to divide us, often along political party lines. Here are a few of the issues that divide Americans today, in an image based on Benjamin Franklin's 1754 political cartoon, "Join, or Die."

Black Americans, women, and the LGBTQ community are just a few groups continuing the fight for equal opportunities.

Democrats favor stronger gun laws, while the majority of Republicans support limited regulation of gun ownership.

We are a nation of immigrants, but immigration policy has always been an issue.

Today, most Republicans say that reducing illegal immigration is a top foreign-policy priority for the country.

EQUALITY

GUN CONTROL

IMMIGRATION

CLIMATE CHANGE

MONEY

People disagree on whether human activity is responsible for the changing global climate.

77% of Democrats say the earth is getting warmer due to human activity.

23% of Republicans say the earth is getting warmer due to human activity.

Whether it's taxes, jobs, or business profits, Americans have strong opinions about money.

84% of Democrats support higher taxes on large businesses.

50% of Republicans support higher taxes on large businesses.

People disagree about America's role in world affairs.

More Democrats than Republicans favor diplomacy over military strength to ensure world peace.

Not all Republicans and Democrats necessarily share these views.

HEALTH CARE

THE WORLD

THE ROLE OF GOVERNMENT

A majority of Americans believe that affordable health care is a major problem facing the United States.

Overall, Democrats think that the government should be responsible for providing affordable health care, while Republicans do not.

This is often what political debate boils down to: What role should the government play in our lives?

Overall, Republicans prefer the government to have a limited role in their lives, while Democrats favor a more involved government.

78% of Democrats think the government should be doing more.

71% of Republicans say the government is doing too much.

Voter Turnout

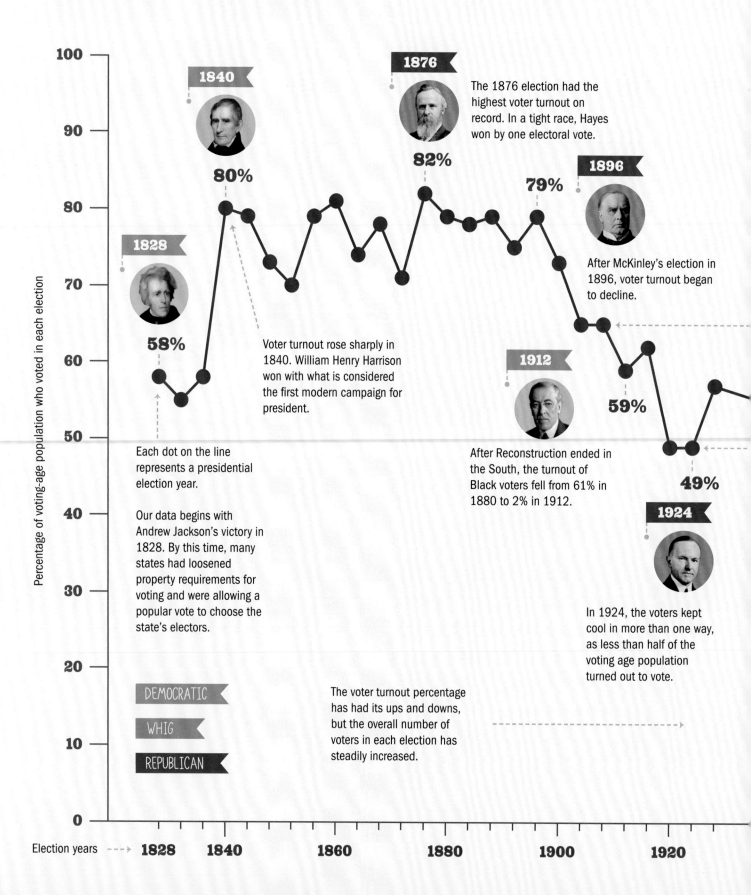

Percentage of voting-age population who voted in each election

1840

80%

1828

58%

1876

The 1876 election had the highest voter turnout on record. In a tight race, Hayes won by one electoral vote.

82%

1896

79%

After McKinley's election in 1896, voter turnout began to decline.

1912

59%

1924

49%

Voter turnout rose sharply in 1840. William Henry Harrison won with what is considered the first modern campaign for president.

Each dot on the line represents a presidential election year.

Our data begins with Andrew Jackson's victory in 1828. By this time, many states had loosened property requirements for voting and were allowing a popular vote to choose the state's electors.

After Reconstruction ended in the South, the turnout of Black voters fell from 61% in 1880 to 2% in 1912.

In 1924, the voters kept cool in more than one way, as less than half of the voting age population turned out to vote.

DEMOCRATIC

WHIG

REPUBLICAN

The voter turnout percentage has had its ups and downs, but the overall number of voters in each election has steadily increased.

Election years ---> **1828**   **1840**   **1860**   **1880**   **1900**   **1920**

People have fought for the right to vote throughout our history. But a significant number of Americans don't get out to vote. Voter turnout is a measurement of the percentage of the voting-age population that shows up to vote. High voter turnout is often cited as evidence of a strong democracy.

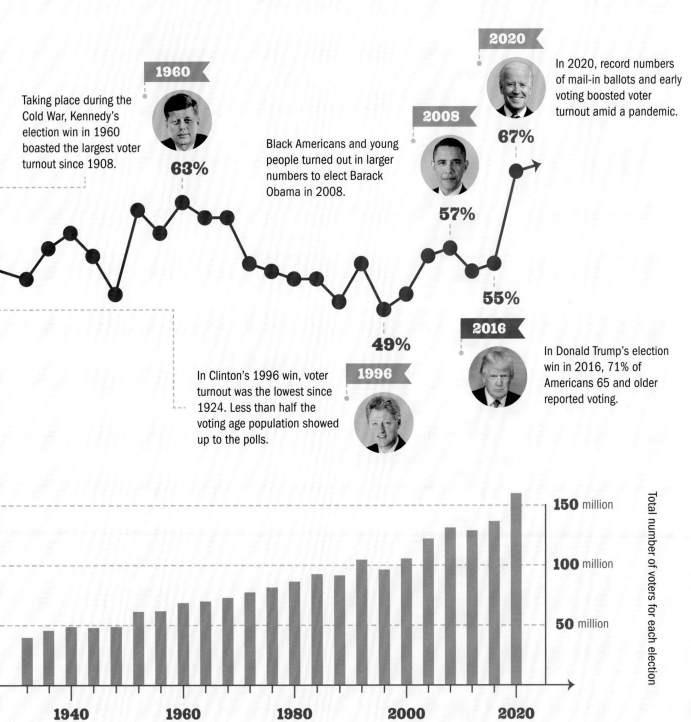

1960

Taking place during the Cold War, Kennedy's election win in 1960 boasted the largest voter turnout since 1908.

63%

2008

Black Americans and young people turned out in larger numbers to elect Barack Obama in 2008.

57%

2020

In 2020, record numbers of mail-in ballots and early voting boosted voter turnout amid a pandemic.

67%

55%

49%

1996

In Clinton's 1996 win, voter turnout was the lowest since 1924. Less than half the voting age population showed up to the polls.

2016

In Donald Trump's election win in 2016, 71% of Americans 65 and older reported voting.

150 million

100 million

50 million

Total number of voters for each election

1940   1960   1980   2000   2020

Presidential Election Firsts

Presidential elections are full of interesting moments with unexpected twists and turns. Follow the path to learn about the groundbreaking elections that have shaped the American presidency.

1789

WASHINGTON FOR PRESIDENT

GENERAL OF THE AMERICAN REVOLUTION

Election year

First presidential election
In the first election under our new government, George Washington was elected unanimously.

1800

REVOLUTION OF 1800
JEFFERSON FOR PRESIDENT

First transfer from one party to another
When Thomas Jefferson defeated John Adams, presidential power was transferred from the Federalists to the Democratic-Republicans.

1844

FIRST DARK HORSE
JAMES K. POLK

First dark horse candidate
James K. Polk came out of nowhere to win the 1844 election.

1840

First modern campaign
The Whigs won with William Henry Harrison in a campaign full of rallies, slogans, songs, and plenty of hard cider.

★ TIPPECANOE ★
Wm. H. Harrison
AND TYLER TOO!

1828

FIRST DEMOCRAT
ANDREW JACKSON

First Democratic president
Old Hickory was the first Democratic president, but his party has changed over the years.

1860

LINCOLN FOR PRESIDENT

THE FIRST REPUBLICAN

First Republican president
In 1860, the Republican Party chose Abraham Lincoln as its candidate.

1872

First election in which **Black men** can vote nationwide

The 15th Amendment gave Black men the right to vote; however, some states blocked this right with poll taxes and literacy tests.

1884

First election with over **10 million** votes cast

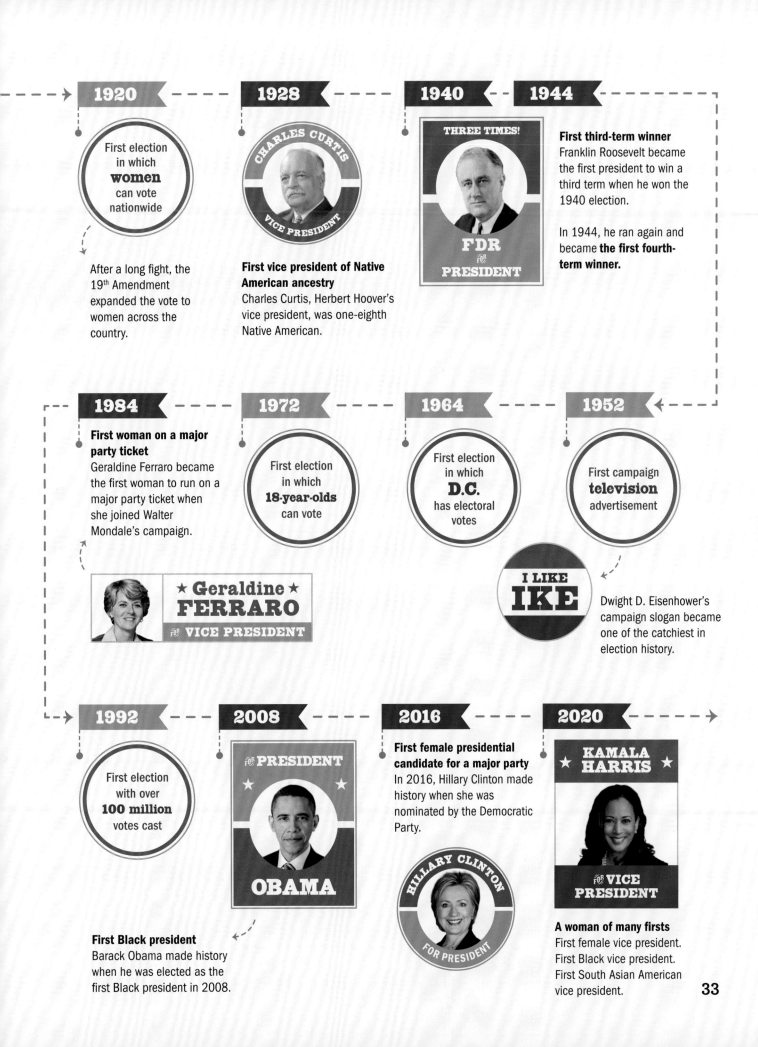

1920

First election in which **women** can vote nationwide

After a long fight, the 19th Amendment expanded the vote to women across the country.

1928

CHARLES CURTIS
VICE PRESIDENT

First vice president of Native American ancestry
Charles Curtis, Herbert Hoover's vice president, was one-eighth Native American.

1940

THREE TIMES!
FDR FOR PRESIDENT

1944

First third-term winner
Franklin Roosevelt became the first president to win a third term when he won the 1940 election.

In 1944, he ran again and became **the first fourth-term winner.**

1984

First woman on a major party ticket
Geraldine Ferraro became the first woman to run on a major party ticket when she joined Walter Mondale's campaign.

★ Geraldine ★ FERRARO FOR VICE PRESIDENT

1972

First election in which **18-year-olds** can vote

1964

First election in which **D.C.** has electoral votes

1952

First campaign **television** advertisement

I LIKE IKE

Dwight D. Eisenhower's campaign slogan became one of the catchiest in election history.

1992

First election with over **100 million** votes cast

2008

FOR PRESIDENT
OBAMA

First Black president
Barack Obama made history when he was elected as the first Black president in 2008.

2016

First female presidential candidate for a major party
In 2016, Hillary Clinton made history when she was nominated by the Democratic Party.

HILLARY CLINTON FOR PRESIDENT

2020

KAMALA HARRIS
FOR VICE PRESIDENT

A woman of many firsts
First female vice president.
First Black vice president.
First South Asian American vice president.

33

Famous First Words

The day the newly elected president takes office is called Inauguration Day. On this day, the president addresses the American people as their chief executive. The words they say can inspire hope or mend a nation after a hard-fought election.

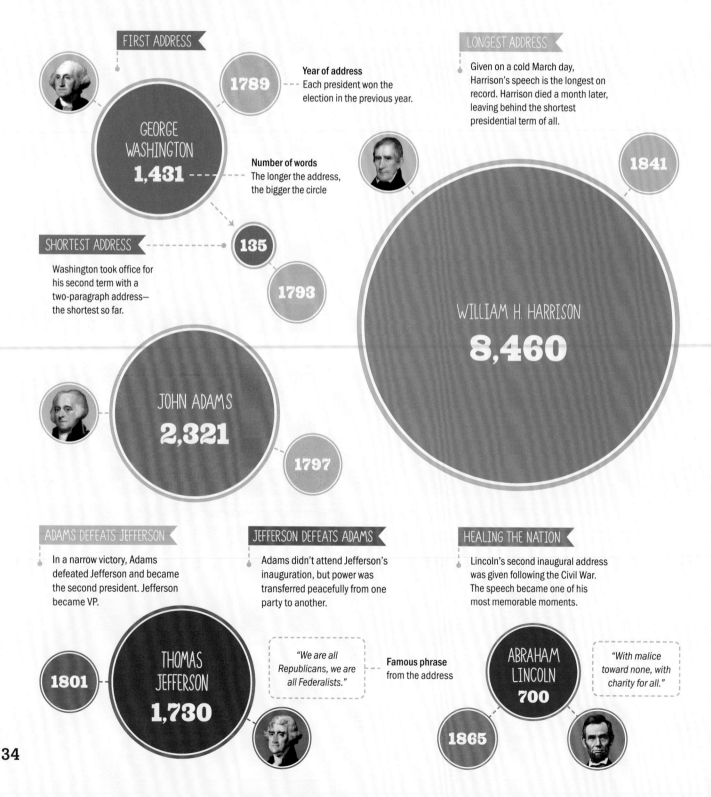

FIRST ADDRESS

Year of address
Each president won the election in the previous year.

GEORGE WASHINGTON
1,431

1789

Number of words
The longer the address, the bigger the circle

SHORTEST ADDRESS

Washington took office for his second term with a two-paragraph address—the shortest so far.

135

1793

LONGEST ADDRESS

Given on a cold March day, Harrison's speech is the longest on record. Harrison died a month later, leaving behind the shortest presidential term of all.

1841

WILLIAM H. HARRISON
8,460

JOHN ADAMS
2,321

1797

ADAMS DEFEATS JEFFERSON

In a narrow victory, Adams defeated Jefferson and became the second president. Jefferson became VP.

JEFFERSON DEFEATS ADAMS

Adams didn't attend Jefferson's inauguration, but power was transferred peacefully from one party to another.

HEALING THE NATION

Lincoln's second inaugural address was given following the Civil War. The speech became one of his most memorable moments.

1801

THOMAS JEFFERSON
1,730

"We are all Republicans, we are all Federalists."

Famous phrase
from the address

ABRAHAM LINCOLN
700

"With malice toward none, with charity for all."

1865

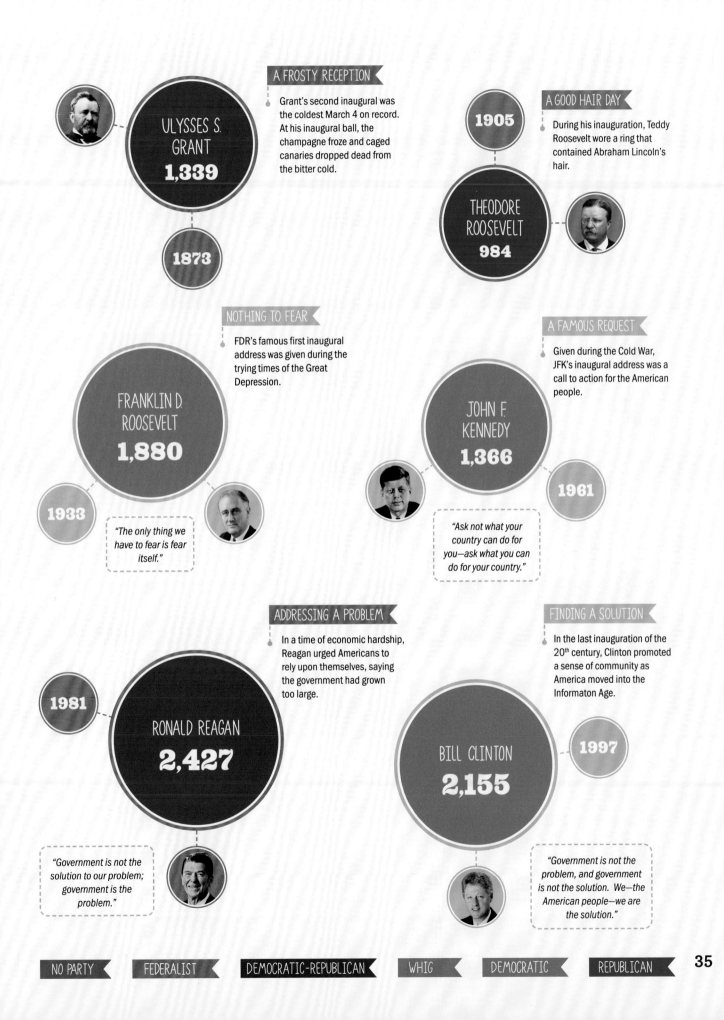

A FROSTY RECEPTION

Grant's second inaugural was the coldest March 4 on record. At his inaugural ball, the champagne froze and caged canaries dropped dead from the bitter cold.

ULYSSES S. GRANT
1,339

1873

1905

A GOOD HAIR DAY

During his inauguration, Teddy Roosevelt wore a ring that contained Abraham Lincoln's hair.

THEODORE ROOSEVELT
984

NOTHING TO FEAR

FDR's famous first inaugural address was given during the trying times of the Great Depression.

FRANKLIN D. ROOSEVELT
1,880

1933

"The only thing we have to fear is fear itself."

A FAMOUS REQUEST

Given during the Cold War, JFK's inaugural address was a call to action for the American people.

JOHN F. KENNEDY
1,366

1961

"Ask not what your country can do for you—ask what you can do for your country."

ADDRESSING A PROBLEM

In a time of economic hardship, Reagan urged Americans to rely upon themselves, saying the government had grown too large.

1981

RONALD REAGAN
2,427

"Government is not the solution to our problem; government is the problem."

FINDING A SOLUTION

In the last inauguration of the 20th century, Clinton promoted a sense of community as America moved into the Informaton Age.

1997

BILL CLINTON
2,155

"Government is not the problem, and government is not the solution. We—the American people—we are the solution."

NO PARTY   FEDERALIST   DEMOCRATIC-REPUBLICAN   WHIG   DEMOCRATIC   REPUBLICAN

In The Headlines

Elections are big news, and some have created quite a stir. It's no secret that the popular vote and the electoral vote have a complicated relationship. The outcomes of elections have ended up in the hands of the House of Representatives, a special election commission, and even the Supreme Court. Here are some elections that made headlines.

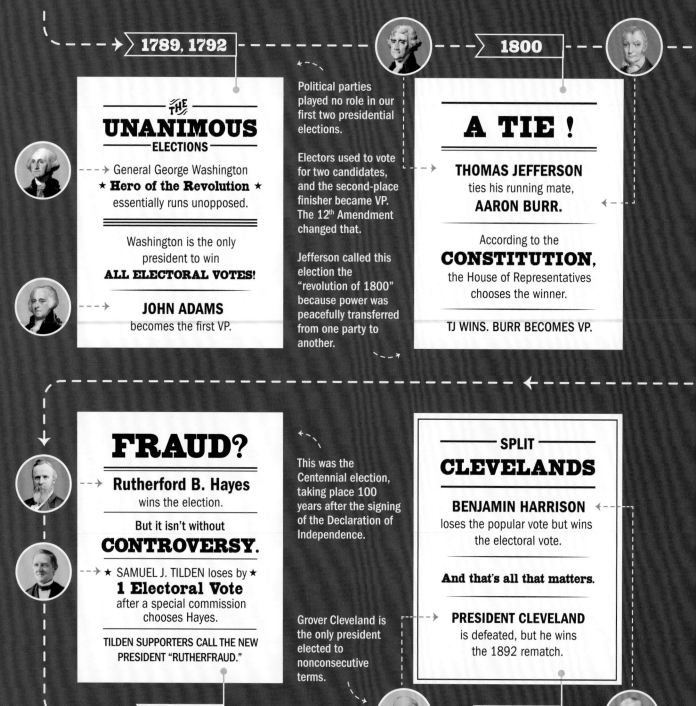

1789, 1792

THE UNANIMOUS ELECTIONS

→ General George Washington
★ **Hero of the Revolution** ★
essentially runs unopposed.

Washington is the only president to win
ALL ELECTORAL VOTES!

→ **JOHN ADAMS**
becomes the first VP.

Political parties played no role in our first two presidential elections.

Electors used to vote for two candidates, and the second-place finisher became VP. The 12th Amendment changed that.

Jefferson called this election the "revolution of 1800" because power was peacefully transferred from one party to another.

1800

A TIE !

THOMAS JEFFERSON
ties his running mate,
AARON BURR.

According to the
CONSTITUTION,
the House of Representatives chooses the winner.

TJ WINS. BURR BECOMES VP.

1876

FRAUD?

→ **Rutherford B. Hayes**
wins the election.

But it isn't without
CONTROVERSY.

→ ★ SAMUEL J. TILDEN loses by ★
1 Electoral Vote
after a special commission chooses Hayes.

TILDEN SUPPORTERS CALL THE NEW PRESIDENT "RUTHERFRAUD."

This was the Centennial election, taking place 100 years after the signing of the Declaration of Independence.

Grover Cleveland is the only president elected to nonconsecutive terms.

1888

SPLIT CLEVELANDS

BENJAMIN HARRISON
loses the popular vote but wins the electoral vote.

And that's all that matters.

→ **PRESIDENT CLEVELAND**
is defeated, but he wins the 1892 rematch.

In the elections with white flags, a candidate lost the popular vote but still won the election. This has happened five times.

POLITICAL PARTIES

No party

Democratic-Republican

Democratic

Republican

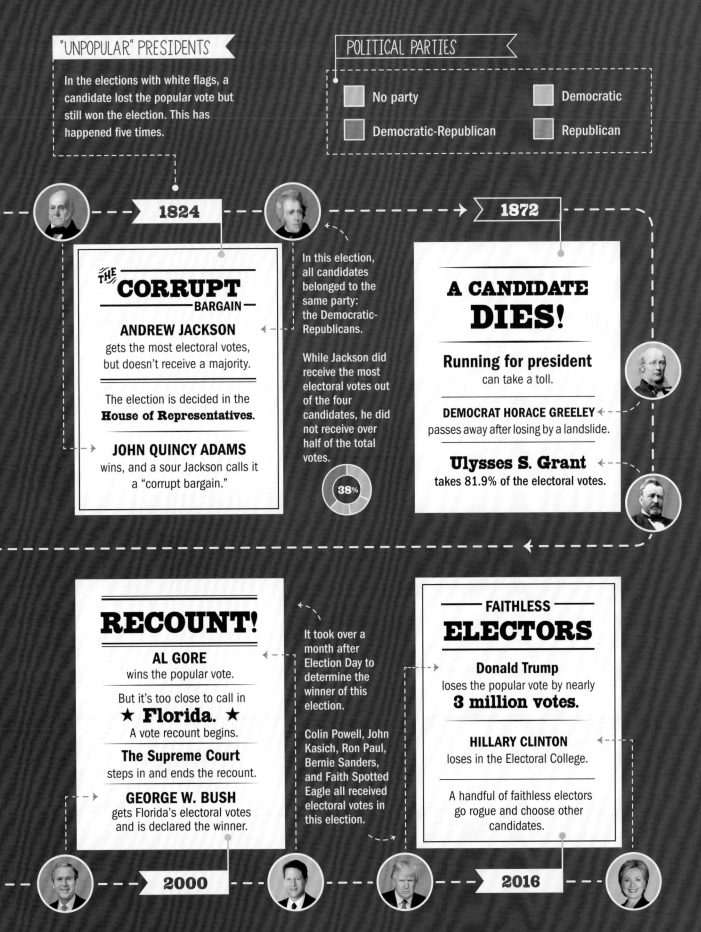

1824

THE CORRUPT BARGAIN

ANDREW JACKSON

gets the most electoral votes, but doesn't receive a majority.

The election is decided in the **House of Representatives.**

JOHN QUINCY ADAMS

wins, and a sour Jackson calls it a "corrupt bargain."

In this election, all candidates belonged to the same party: the Democratic-Republicans.

While Jackson did receive the most electoral votes out of the four candidates, he did not receive over half of the total votes.

38%

1872

A CANDIDATE DIES!

Running for president
can take a toll.

DEMOCRAT HORACE GREELEY
passes away after losing by a landslide.

Ulysses S. Grant
takes 81.9% of the electoral votes.

RECOUNT!

AL GORE
wins the popular vote.

But it's too close to call in
★ **Florida.** ★
A vote recount begins.

The Supreme Court
steps in and ends the recount.

GEORGE W. BUSH
gets Florida's electoral votes and is declared the winner.

It took over a month after Election Day to determine the winner of this election.

Colin Powell, John Kasich, Ron Paul, Bernie Sanders, and Faith Spotted Eagle all received electoral votes in this election.

FAITHLESS ELECTORS

Donald Trump
loses the popular vote by nearly
3 million votes.

HILLARY CLINTON
loses in the Electoral College.

A handful of faithless electors go rogue and choose other candidates.

2000

2016

John Adams called the vice presidency "the most insignificant office that ever the invention of man contrived." But Adams could not have foreseen its historical impact. Here are the nine men who accidentally ascended to the presidency.

1841

JOHN TYLER

William Henry Harrison's death sparked a debate over how the vice president took over the duties of the office. The Constitution was unclear, and the Framers were no longer around to ask.

John Tyler wasted no time in becoming the new president. He even refused letters addressed to him as "acting president" of the United States.

MILLARD FILLMORE

1850

Sticking with the precedent set by Tyler, Fillmore ascended to the presidency after Zachary Taylor's unexpected death.

THE
Accidental Bond

ANDREW JOHNSON

1865

Johnson had big shoes to fill after Abraham Lincoln's assassination. Unfortunately, Johnson proved to be an ineffective leader during the pivotal time following the Civil War.

CHESTER A. ARTHUR

1881

For eighty days, James Garfield fought to survive after being injured by an assassin's bullet. A reluctant Arthur took over the office only after Garfield died.

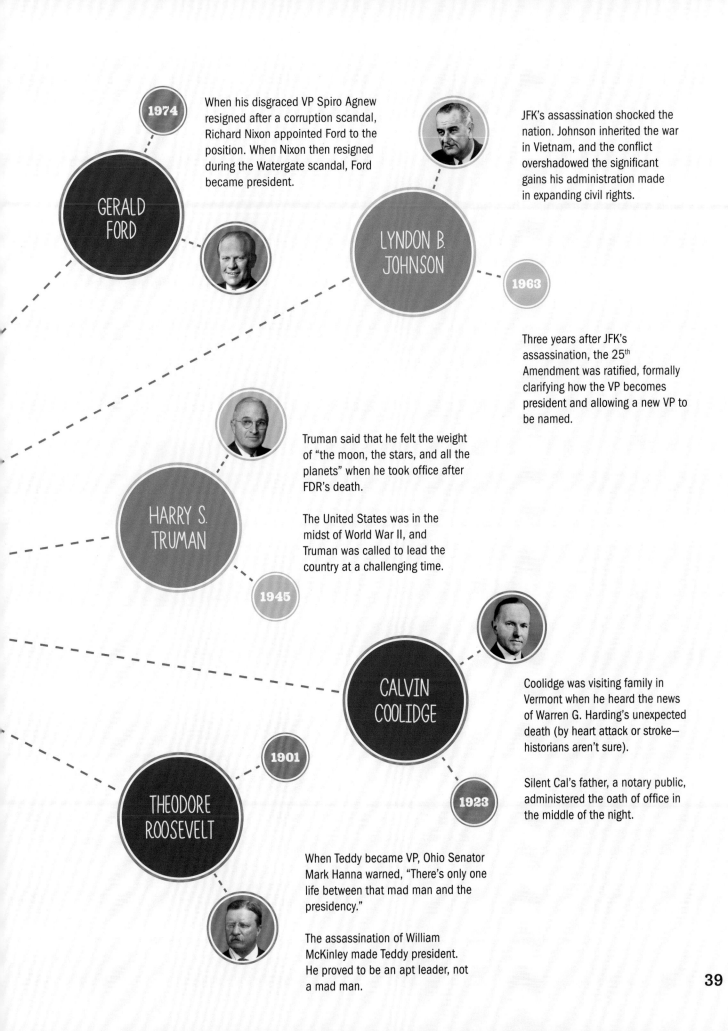

1974 When his disgraced VP Spiro Agnew resigned after a corruption scandal, Richard Nixon appointed Ford to the position. When Nixon then resigned during the Watergate scandal, Ford became president.

GERALD FORD

JFK's assassination shocked the nation. Johnson inherited the war in Vietnam, and the conflict overshadowed the significant gains his administration made in expanding civil rights.

LYNDON B. JOHNSON

1963

Three years after JFK's assassination, the 25th Amendment was ratified, formally clarifying how the VP becomes president and allowing a new VP to be named.

Truman said that he felt the weight of "the moon, the stars, and all the planets" when he took office after FDR's death.

HARRY S. TRUMAN

The United States was in the midst of World War II, and Truman was called to lead the country at a challenging time.

1945

CALVIN COOLIDGE

Coolidge was visiting family in Vermont when he heard the news of Warren G. Harding's unexpected death (by heart attack or stroke—historians aren't sure).

Silent Cal's father, a notary public, administered the oath of office in the middle of the night.

1901

1923

THEODORE ROOSEVELT

When Teddy became VP, Ohio Senator Mark Hanna warned, "There's only one life between that mad man and the presidency."

The assassination of William McKinley made Teddy president. He proved to be an apt leader, not a mad man.

Lines *of* Communication

My fellow Americans: Today, we live in a world where the president instantly communicates with millions of people. This hasn't always been the case. See how our lines of communication have changed over time.

THE TELEPHONE

In June 1877, Rutherford B. Hayes became the first president to use a phone. He had the "wonderful" device installed in the White House that fall. Its number? 1.

1876

Alexander Graham Bell is issued the first U.S. patent for the telephone.

1920

Percentage of American households with a telephone

35%

1844

Telegraph inventor Samuel Morse sends his famous message "What hath God wrought" from Washington, D.C., to Baltimore.

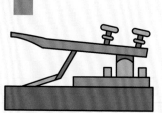

THE NEWSPAPER

In January 1790, newspapers printed George Washington's first State of the Union address and informed readers of the president's attire.

1784

America's first daily newspaper, the *Pennsylvania Packet and Daily Advertiser*, is published.

THE TELEGRAPH

During the Civil War, Abraham Lincoln used the telegraph in the War Department building to receive news of battles.

The first White House telegraph was installed in 1866 during Andrew Johnson's presidency.

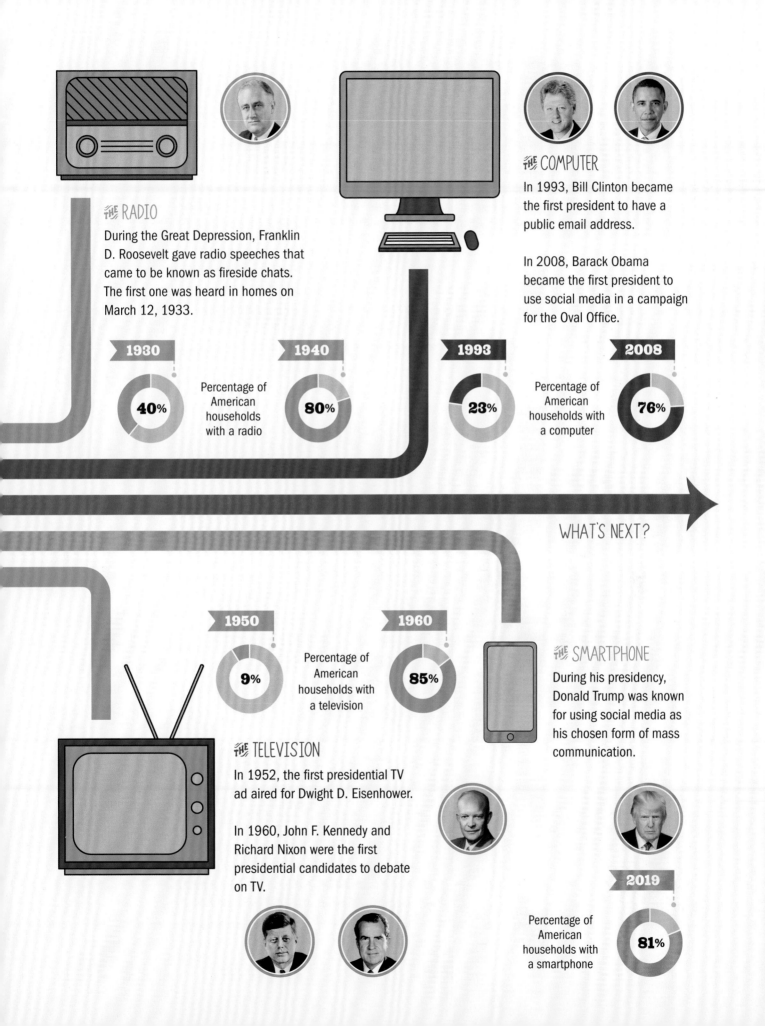

THE RADIO

During the Great Depression, Franklin D. Roosevelt gave radio speeches that came to be known as fireside chats. The first one was heard in homes on March 12, 1933.

1930

40%

Percentage of American households with a radio

1940

80%

THE COMPUTER

In 1993, Bill Clinton became the first president to have a public email address.

In 2008, Barack Obama became the first president to use social media in a campaign for the Oval Office.

1993

23%

Percentage of American households with a computer

2008

76%

WHAT'S NEXT?

1950

9%

Percentage of American households with a television

1960

85%

THE TELEVISION

In 1952, the first presidential TV ad aired for Dwight D. Eisenhower.

In 1960, John F. Kennedy and Richard Nixon were the first presidential candidates to debate on TV.

THE SMARTPHONE

During his presidency, Donald Trump was known for using social media as his chosen form of mass communication.

2019

81%

Percentage of American households with a smartphone

Mail TO THE Chief

Writing to the president is one way for your voice to be heard. As president, Thomas Jefferson received about 140 items in the mail each month. By the time Barack Obama took office, the White House received about 65,000 letters per week. Let's read a few memorable letters mailed to our chief executive.

TO...THE PRESIDENT

The lands we justly own as a nation are taken from us; we shall thus be deprived of our inheritance without our consent. We pray that you will not suffer this wrong to be done to us.

MUHHECONNUK

November 16, 1819

A Plea from the Muhheconnuk

The Muhheconnuk were one of the Native American nations to protest the forced removal from their lands. In this case, they asked President Monroe to return land that was given to the Delaware Nation.

October 15, 1860

A Young Girl's Advice

Before Abraham Lincoln was known for his famous beard, 11-year-old Grace Bedell wrote the presidential candidate telling him that he should grow whiskers.

DEAR SIR

I have got 4 brother's and part of them will vote for you any way and if you will let your whiskers grow I will try and get the rest of them to vote for you you would look a great deal better for your face is so thin.

GRACE BEDELL

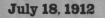

HONORED SIR:

I am asking you . . . to secure the right of every qualified . . . voter in the State of Oklahoma and especially in the city of Tulsa, Okla. to vote in the coming elections . . .

VERY TRULY YOURS,
C. DEARMAN

July 18, 1912

A Businessman's Urgent Request

Even after being granted the right to vote, Black Americans in many states fought for equal access to voting. In this letter, a Tulsa businessman asks President Taft to ensure that Black men such as himself can cast their ballots.

August 2, 1939

A Scientist's Warning

Immediately before the outbreak of World War II, Albert Einstein warned Franklin D. Roosevelt of a new technology that used uranium. Six years later, the United States developed the first atomic bomb.

SIR:

Some recent work . . . leads me to expect that the element uranium may be turned into a new and important source of energy in the immediate future . . .

This new phenomenon would also lead to the construction of bombs . . .

YOURS VERY TRULY,
A. EINSTEIN

MR. TRUMAN

As you have been directly responsible for the loss of our son's life in Korea, you might just as well keep this emblem on display in your trophy room, as a memory of one of your historic deeds.

WILLIAM BANNING

c. 1953

A Grievance from a Father

After his son's death in the Korean War, William Banning sent former president Truman a letter enclosed with his son's Purple Heart medal. The letter and medal were discovered in Truman's desk after his death in 1972.

May 13, 1958

An Athlete on Civil Rights

After President Dwight D. Eisenhower explained that civil rights would come with patience, Jackie Robinson, the man who broke the color barrier in Major League Baseball in 1947, wrote the president a letter.

MY DEAR MR. PRESIDENT:

I respectfully remind you sir, that we have been the most patient of all people . . .

We want to enjoy now the rights that we feel we are entitled to as Americans.

RESPECTFULLY YOURS,
JACKIE ROBINSON

DEAR MR. PRESIDENT,

Today my mother declared my bedroom a disaster area. I would like to request federal funds to hire a crew to clean up my room.

SINCERELY YOURS,
ANDY SMITH

April 18, 1984

A Boy's Humorous Request

In this letter, Andy Smith requested President Ronald Reagan's help. Reagan wrote back suggesting Andy should "practice volunteerism" to solve his problem.

You can write to the president too!

THE WHITE HOUSE
1600 PENNSYLVANIA AVE. NW
WASHINGTON, D.C. 20500

Challenging the President

Sometimes the people and the president disagree. For many years, women fought for the right to vote. When President Woodrow Wilson was slow to offer his support, women responded by picketing outside the White House. They used banners such as this to peacefully protest and to create change.

INTERPRETING THE BANNER

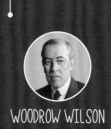

WOODROW WILSON

Leaders of the women's suffrage movement met with President Wilson seeking his endorsement of women's right to vote. But he told them, "You can afford a little while to wait." In response, women picketed the White House in January 1917, holding this banner.

ALICE PAUL

Alice Paul and other members of the National Woman's Party were arrested and jailed as their picketing of the White House continued for months.

The arrests happened nearly seventy years after Elizabeth Cady Stanton and Lucretia Mott led the first U.S. women's rights convention in Seneca Falls, New York, in 1848.

ELIZABETH CADY STANTON

With the ratification of the 19th Amendment in 1920, women gained the right to vote nationwide. This was a major milestone in women's fight for liberty.

LUCRETIA MOTT

In 2017, just after the inauguration of Donald Trump—one hundred years after this banner was carried—women organized what is thought to be the largest single-day protest in history: the Women's March on Washington. In addition to gathering in D.C., women throughout the world joined in with rallies in support of gender equality.

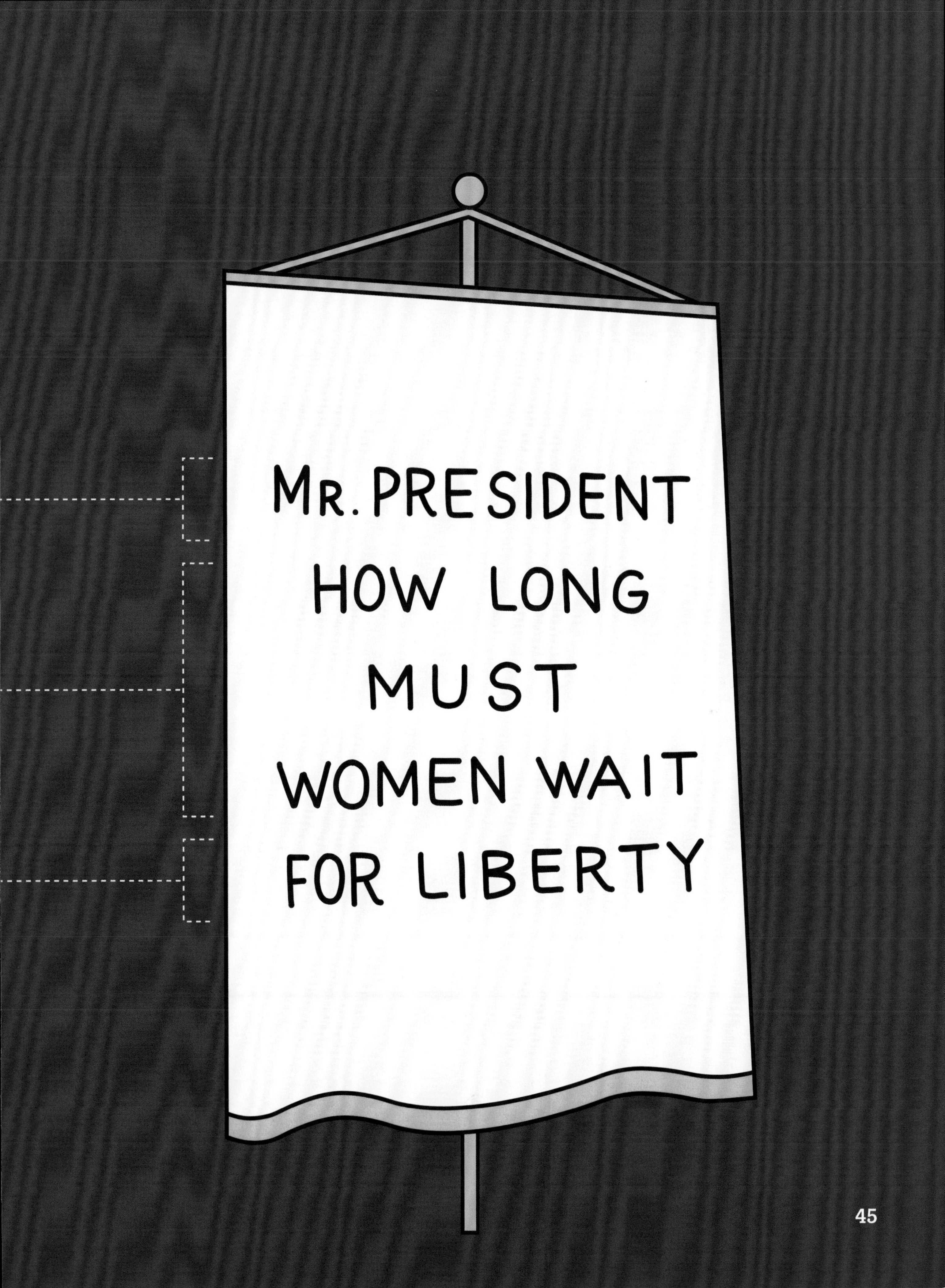
MR. PRESIDENT
HOW LONG
MUST
WOMEN WAIT
FOR LIBERTY

Will we continue to expand the vote?

Recent efforts focus on improving voting access for all citizens.

26TH AMENDMENT
1971

Ratified during the Vietnam War, the 26th Amendment lowered the voting age to 18.

About 4 million Americans turn 18 each year.

VOTING RIGHTS ACT
1965

The act stops discriminatory practices used by states to limit the voting of Black Americans and others.

In 1968, Shirley Chisholm became the first Black woman elected to Congress.

24TH AMENDMENT
1964

States can no longer require voters to pay a tax in order to vote in federal elections.

Because of obstacles to voting, only an estimated 3% of eligible Black voters were registered in the South by 1940.

23RD AMENDMENT
1961

Residents of Washington, D.C., can now vote in presidential elections.

Washington, D.C., has three electoral votes in a presidential election.

McCARRAN–WALTER ACT
1952

This act removed barriers to citizenship for Asian immigrants, but limited their entry into the United States.

This immigration law opened the door for voting, but also established quotas based on race.

INDIAN CITIZENSHIP ACT
1924

This act granted citizenship to all Native Americans born in the United States, but states still denied their right to vote.

Despite the 15th Amendment, 33 years passed before Native American citizens could vote in every state.

19TH AMENDMENT
1920

This amendment guarantees women's right to vote.

Since 1980, women have turned out to vote for president at greater rates than men.

Expanding We the People

The Constitution begins with the words "We the People." When it was written, the people who could vote resembled the Founders: white, wealthy, and male. With each new act or amendment, the voting population has grown to include more Americans.

WHAT IS IT?

DID YOU KNOW?

END of PROPERTY REQUIREMENTS
1888

Property ownership was once required to vote. Men who owned property were thought to have a stake in society.

In 1888, Rhode Island was the last state to end property requirements. At this time, most white men could vote.

15TH AMENDMENT
1870

This amendment says a citizen's right to vote cannot be denied based on race, but states found ways around it.

Hiram Revels became the first Black senator—just three weeks after this amendment was ratified.

14TH AMENDMENT
1868

The 14th Amendment guaranteed citizenship and equal protection of the law for all citizens and set the voting age at 21.

Congress added this definition to the Constitution so future laws could not redefine citizenship.

CIVIL RIGHTS ACT
1866

This act granted citizenship to everyone born in the United States except Native Americans.

By the end of 1868, registered Black voters outnumbered registered white voters in the South.

U.S. CONSTITUTION
1787

The Constitution doesn't mention voting requirements, so it was left up to the states to decide.

It's estimated that about 12% of the American population could vote in the first presidential election.

Obstacles to Voting

Voting is an important part of a healthy democracy. However, throughout history obstacles have blocked the right to vote for some Americans.

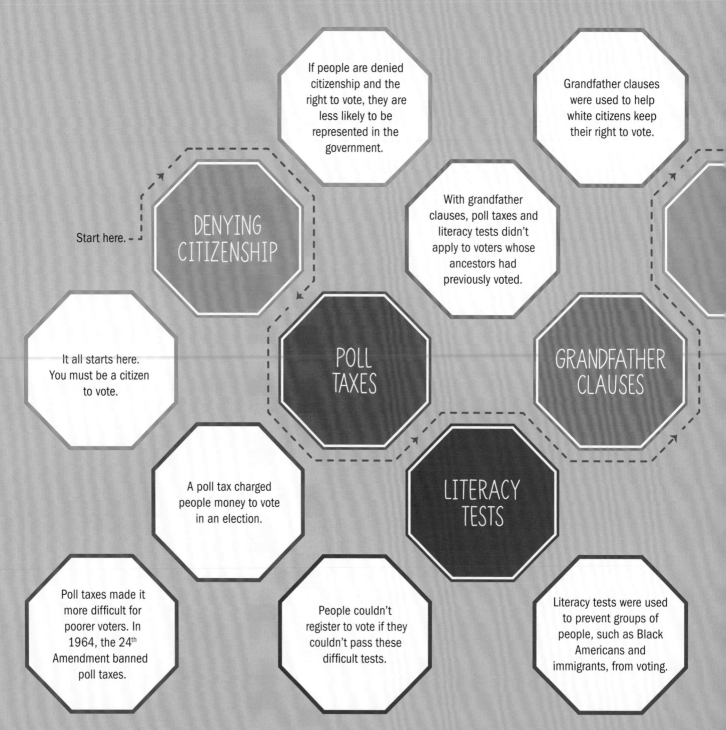

If people are denied citizenship and the right to vote, they are less likely to be represented in the government.

Grandfather clauses were used to help white citizens keep their right to vote.

Start here.

DENYING CITIZENSHIP

With grandfather clauses, poll taxes and literacy tests didn't apply to voters whose ancestors had previously voted.

It all starts here. You must be a citizen to vote.

POLL TAXES

GRANDFATHER CLAUSES

A poll tax charged people money to vote in an election.

LITERACY TESTS

Poll taxes made it more difficult for poorer voters. In 1964, the 24th Amendment banned poll taxes.

People couldn't register to vote if they couldn't pass these difficult tests.

Literacy tests were used to prevent groups of people, such as Black Americans and immigrants, from voting.

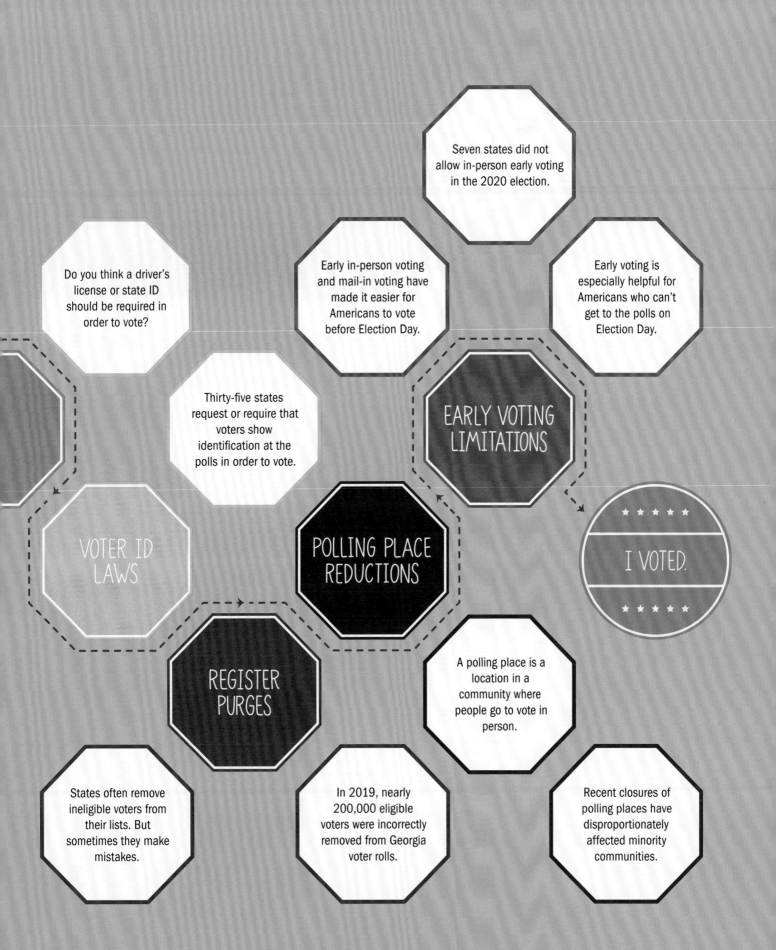

Seven states did not allow in-person early voting in the 2020 election.

Do you think a driver's license or state ID should be required in order to vote?

Early in-person voting and mail-in voting have made it easier for Americans to vote before Election Day.

Early voting is especially helpful for Americans who can't get to the polls on Election Day.

Thirty-five states request or require that voters show identification at the polls in order to vote.

EARLY VOTING LIMITATIONS

I VOTED.

VOTER ID LAWS

POLLING PLACE REDUCTIONS

REGISTER PURGES

A polling place is a location in a community where people go to vote in person.

States often remove ineligible voters from their lists. But sometimes they make mistakes.

In 2019, nearly 200,000 eligible voters were incorrectly removed from Georgia voter rolls.

Recent closures of polling places have disproportionately affected minority communities.

THE Gerrymander

This is the gerrymander, a creature that represents the outlandish shapes of congressional districts. Every ten years, the Census measures population, and districts are redrawn to reflect the change in numbers. Some districts are gerrymandered into unnatural shapes to favor one party over the other.

This monster image is from an 1812 political cartoon, "The Gerry-Mander," ridiculing a salamander-shaped district approved by Massachusetts governor Elbridge Gerry.

WHAT IS A DISTRICT?

States are divided into congressional districts based on population. Each district has about 760,000 people, who elect one House of Representatives member to represent them in Congress. Wyoming, the least populated state, has one district, while California, the most populated state, has fifty-two districts.

1
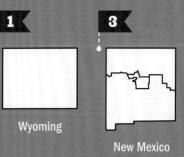
Wyoming

3
New Mexico

52

California

WHAT DOES IT LOOK LIKE TODAY?

If a state doesn't have strict rules on how lines are drawn, new districts may be created to favor one party over the other—making monstrous districts like this:

THE DUCK
Ohio's 4th District

THE PTERODACTYL
Maryland's 6th District

THE UPSIDE-DOWN ELEPHANT
Texas's 35th District

SEE HOW IT WORKS

Below, you'll see a group of 25 voters divided three different ways. See how changing the boundaries of a district affects who wins in each situation.

1
Blue wins two districts 5–0.

2

3
Red wins 5–0.   *Blue wins 4–1.*

Blue wins 3–2.

Red wins three districts 5–0.   *Red wins all districts 3–2.*   *Red wins 5–0.*   *Blue wins 3–2.*

25 total voters
15 red (60%)
10 blue (40%)

Red voters are the majority before the group is divided into districts.

The five districts are drawn equally in vertical columns.

Red wins 3 districts.
Blue wins 2 districts.

The five districts are drawn equally in horizontal rows—to red's advantage.

Red wins 5 districts.
Blue wins no districts.

The five districts are gerrymandered to blue's advantage.

Red wins 2 districts.
Blue wins 3 districts.

Seeking Approval

The job of the president has its ups and downs. Since 1938, these fluctuations have been measured by Gallup, a company known for its opinion polls. Every week, Gallup surveys the feelings of the American people, and job approval ratings are posted. Sometimes the political climate can negatively impact approval. At other times, a well-handled disaster or a major rallying event can boost ratings.

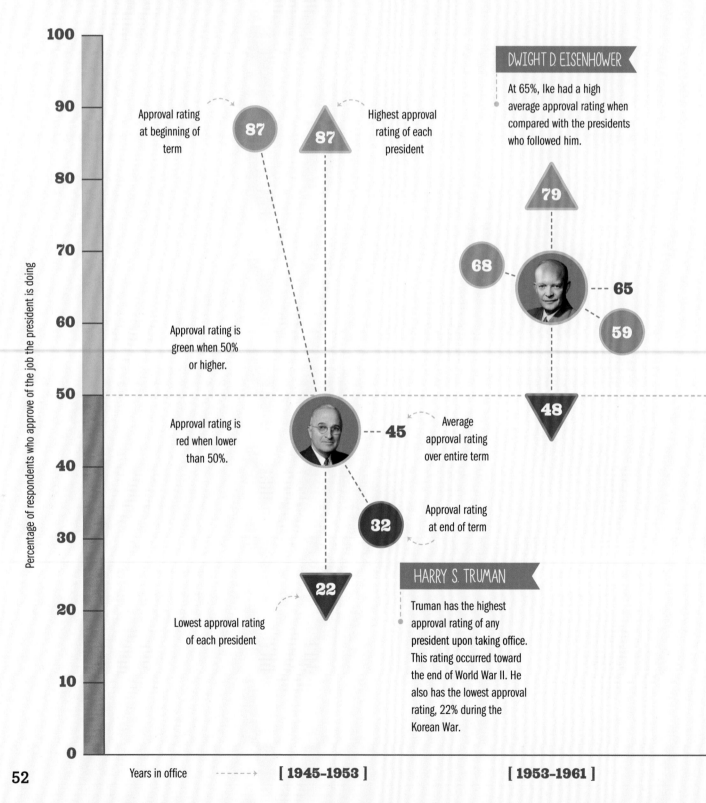

Percentage of respondents who approve of the job the president is doing

Approval rating at beginning of term — 87

Highest approval rating of each president — 87

Approval rating is green when 50% or higher.

Approval rating is red when lower than 50%.

45 — Average approval rating over entire term

32 — Approval rating at end of term

Lowest approval rating of each president — 22

DWIGHT D. EISENHOWER

At 65%, Ike had a high average approval rating when compared with the presidents who followed him.

HARRY S. TRUMAN

Truman has the highest approval rating of any president upon taking office. This rating occurred toward the end of World War II. He also has the lowest approval rating, 22% during the Korean War.

Years in office

[1945–1953]   [1953–1961]

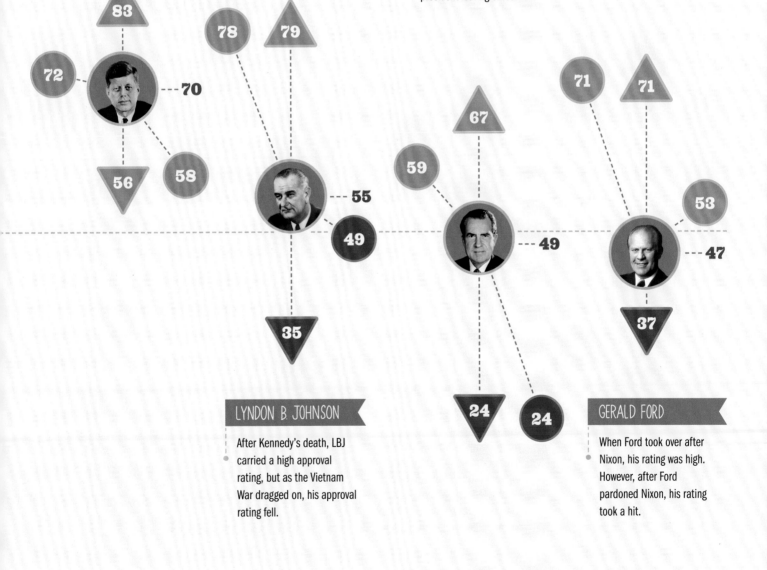

JOHN F. KENNEDY

JFK has the highest average approval rating of all presidents. He's the only president to stay in the green the whole time.

83
78
79
72
70
56
58
55
49

RICHARD NIXON

The people lost faith in the presidency after Nixon's Watergate scandal. At the time of his resignation, Nixon had his lowest approval rating and the lowest rating of any president leaving office.

71
71
67
59
49
53
47
37

35

LYNDON B. JOHNSON

After Kennedy's death, LBJ carried a high approval rating, but as the Vietnam War dragged on, his approval rating fell.

24
24

GERALD FORD

When Ford took over after Nixon, his rating was high. However, after Ford pardoned Nixon, his rating took a hit.

[1961–1963]   [1963–1969]   [1969–1974]   [1974–1977]

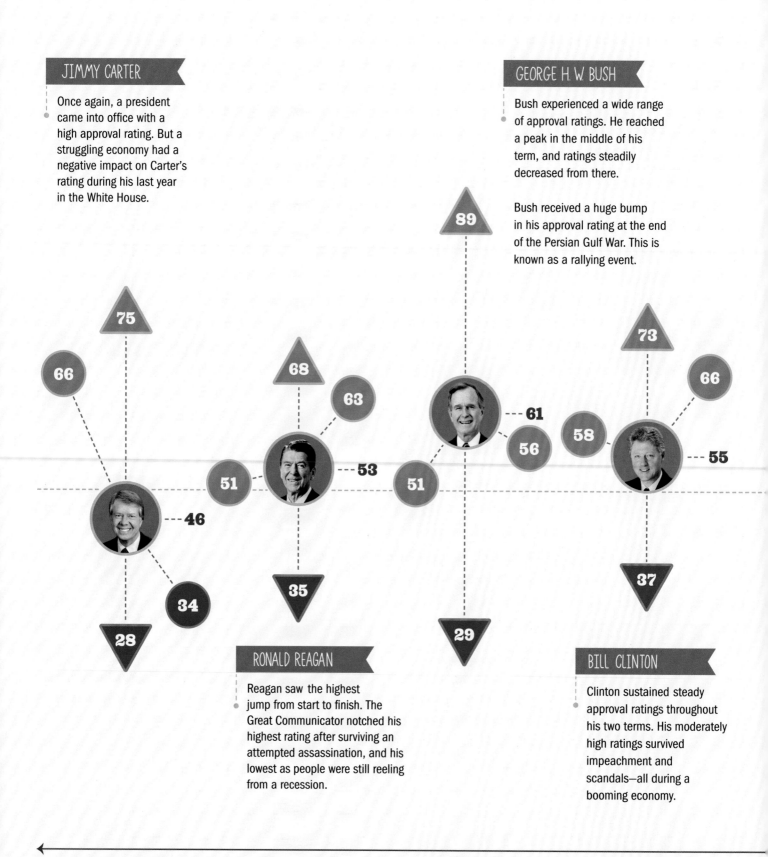

JIMMY CARTER

Once again, a president came into office with a high approval rating. But a struggling economy had a negative impact on Carter's rating during his last year in the White House.

GEORGE H. W. BUSH

Bush experienced a wide range of approval ratings. He reached a peak in the middle of his term, and ratings steadily decreased from there.

Bush received a huge bump in his approval rating at the end of the Persian Gulf War. This is known as a rallying event.

RONALD REAGAN

Reagan saw the highest jump from start to finish. The Great Communicator notched his highest rating after surviving an attempted assassination, and his lowest as people were still reeling from a recession.

BILL CLINTON

Clinton sustained steady approval ratings throughout his two terms. His moderately high ratings survived impeachment and scandals—all during a booming economy.

75
66
68
63
89
73
66
51
53
61
56
58
55
46
51
35
37
34
28
29

[1977-1981]   [1981-1989]   [1989-1993]   [1993-2001]

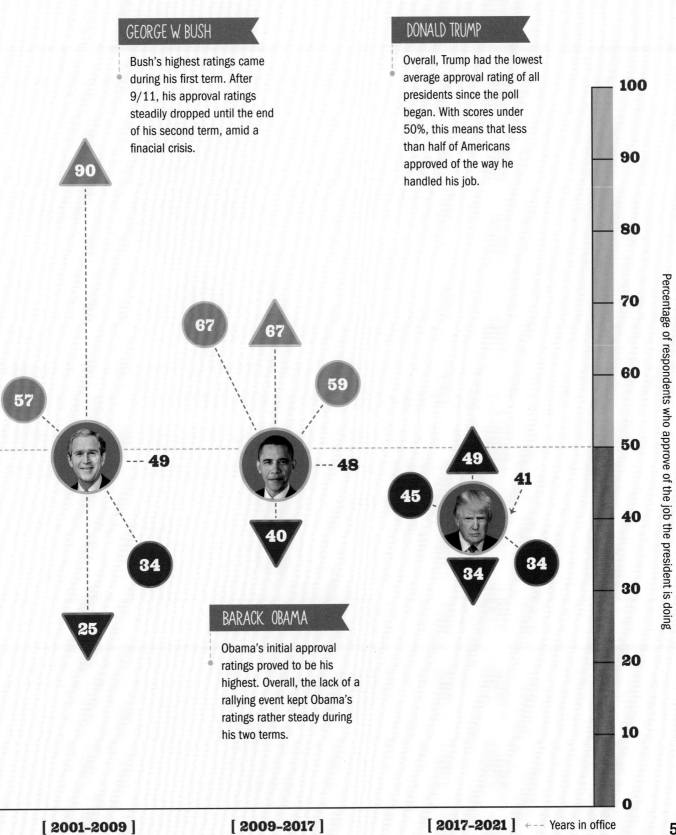

GEORGE W. BUSH

Bush's highest ratings came during his first term. After 9/11, his approval ratings steadily dropped until the end of his second term, amid a finacial crisis.

DONALD TRUMP

Overall, Trump had the lowest average approval rating of all presidents since the poll began. With scores under 50%, this means that less than half of Americans approved of the way he handled his job.

BARACK OBAMA

Obama's initial approval ratings proved to be his highest. Overall, the lack of a rallying event kept Obama's ratings rather steady during his two terms.

90

67   67

57   59

49   48   49   41

45

40   34   34

34

25

Percentage of respondents who approve of the job the president is doing

100
90
80
70
60
50
40
30
20
10
0

[2001-2009]   [2009-2017]   [2017-2021] ← -- Years in office

The Next Chapter

After closing the book on the presidency, former presidents move on to the next chapter of their lives. Which path would you choose?

Teddy Roosevelt, Martin Van Buren, and Millard Fillmore all ran (and lost) on third-party tickets after their presidencies.

RUN AGAIN

After a turbulent presidency, James Buchanan was happy to pass the torch to Abraham Lincoln and retire to Wheatland, his home in Pennsylvania.

LIVE THE QUIET LIFE

Many presidents leave public life and retire to their homes. After serving two terms, George Washington voluntarily left office and returned to his Virginia estate, Mount Vernon.

After a busy public life as a general and a president, Dwight D. Eisenhower found relaxation in painting at his Gettysburg, Pennsylvania, farm.

RETURN TO GOVERNMENT

A handful of presidents continued to serve in the government after they left the White House. John Quincy Adams made a lasting impression during his nine terms in the House of Representatives.

William H. Taft served on the Supreme Court as chief justice of the United States—the only former president to do so.

BUILD YOUR LIBRARY

After leaving office, a president has the opportunity to shape one's legacy by building a presidential library and museum.

Every president since Herbert Hoover has a presidential library overseen by the National Archives.

WRITE YOUR MEMOIRS

Former presidents often write about their experiences in the White House. Despite his quiet nature, Calvin Coolidge had a lot to say in his memoirs.

Ulysses S. Grant wrote his memoirs at the end of his life while battling cancer.

SUPPORT A CAUSE

Sometimes presidents use their influence to promote a cause that's important to them. Thomas Jefferson founded the University of Virginia.

Jimmy Carter has worked tirelessly for human rights, affordable housing, and other charitable causes.

For over 200 years, the American people have worked to keep this republic. Participation is necessary to preserve our democracy. It's a tough task, and we can do it! But don't take our word for it.

"My dear friends, your vote is precious, almost sacred. It is the most powerful nonviolent tool we have to create a more perfect union."

JOHN LEWIS
Congressman, civil rights leader

"A republic, if you can keep it."

BENJAMIN FRANKLIN
Delegate to the Constitutional Convention

"Here, sir, the people govern: Here they act by their immediate representatives."

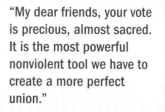

ALEXANDER HAMILTON
Delegate to the Constitutional Convention

We Can

"If there is no struggle, there is no progress."

FREDERICK DOUGLASS
Writer, orator, activist

"What keeps a republic on its legs is good citizenship."

"Government of the people, by the people, for the people, shall not perish from the earth."

MARK TWAIN
Author

ABRAHAM LINCOLN
16th president

"Fight for the things that you care about, but do it in a way that will lead others to join you."

RUTH BADER GINSBURG
Supreme Court justice

"Join me in an effort to reshape our society and regain control of our destiny."

SHIRLEY CHISHOLM
Congresswoman

"This is your democracy—make it—protect it—pass it on."

THURGOOD MARSHALL
Supreme Court justice

Do It!

"The ultimate rulers of our democracy are not a President and Senators and Congressmen and Government officials but the voters of this country."

FRANKLIN D. ROOSEVELT
32nd president

"Organize! Agitate! Educate! must be our war-cry."

"Democracy is not static. It is a living force."

SUSAN B. ANTHONY
Women's rights leader

HERBERT HOOVER
31st president

A Lasting Memory

The National Mall in Washington, D.C., is a space to embrace our history. The memorials, monuments, and museums all preserve a past from which we continue to learn.

The Lincoln Memorial anchors the west end of the National Mall. It's a fitting backdrop to many American stories and a place where the people and the president stand together.

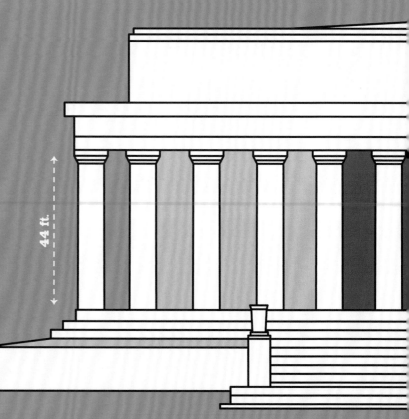

OUR NATION'S MALL

Located in the heart of Washington, D.C., the National Mall is a place where the people go to gather, learn, and relax.

Around the Mall, you'll find the National Archives, a number of Smithsonian museums, and the U.S. Capitol building.

MALL STATS

25,000,000+
visitors per year

70+
monuments and memorials

11
Smithsonian museums and galleries

44 ft.

188 ft.

PEOPLE HONORED

George Washington, Thomas Jefferson, Abraham Lincoln, Ulysses S. Grant, Franklin D. Roosevelt, and Martin Luther King Jr. are honored with memorials or monuments.

The newest memorial on the Mall is dedicated to Dwight D. Eisenhower.

VETERANS REMEMBERED

Those who have served in foreign wars are honored throughout the Mall, with impressive memorials for veterans of World War II, the Korean War, and the Vietnam War. Ground was broken in 2017 on a World War I memorial.

BUILT WITH INTENTION

36 columns
for each state in the Union at the time of Lincoln's death

2 painted murals
entitled *Emancipation* and *Unity*

LINCOLN MEMORIAL STATS

The memorial was dedicated on
May 30, 1922.

Lincoln's statue is
19 feet tall.

The statue is composed of
28 blocks of marble.

The memorial weighs approximately
76,000,000 pounds.

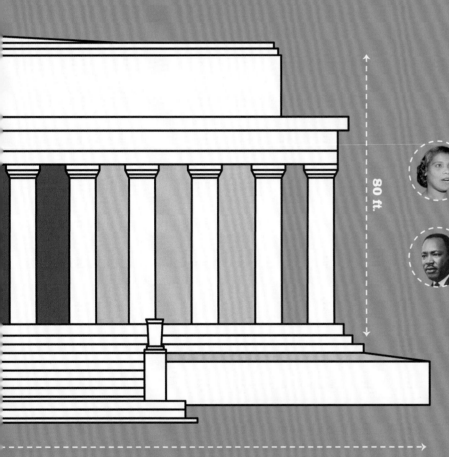

80 ft.

A MEETING PLACE

The Lincoln Memorial has become a gathering place for Americans.

In 1939, Marian Anderson, a revered American singer, performed to a crowd of 75,000 at a memorable concert.

In 1963, over 200,000 people gathered together for racial equality and saw Martin Luther King Jr. give his "I Have a Dream" speech on the steps of the Lincoln Memorial.

WORDS MATTER

Inside you'll find two of Lincoln's most famous speeches: the Gettysburg Address and his Second Inaugural Address. The words are carved into the stone.

LINCOLN LEGEND

Abraham Lincoln is one of our most popular presidents. He led our country through the Civil War and lost his life to an assassin's bullet. People from around the world come to pay their respects to an American hero.

PAST AND FUTURE

We have built monuments and memorials that will last generations. What do our monuments and memorials tell us about the people who came before us? And what memorials will we build in the future?

ᵀᴴᴱ Presidential Yearbook

GEORGE WASHINGTON

Father of His Country
Years in office: 1789–1797
Political party: None, but favored Federalist
Birthday: February 22, 1732
MOST LIKELY TO BECOME PRESIDENT

JOHN ADAMS

Atlas of Independence
Years in office: 1797–1801
Political party: Federalist
Birthday: October 30, 1735
MOST LIKELY TO BECOME A LAWYER

JAMES MONROE

Last Cocked Hat
Years in office: 1817–1825
Political party: Democratic-Republican
Birthday: April 28, 1758
MOST OUTDATED WARDROBE

JOHN QUINCY ADAMS

Old Man Eloquent
Years in office: 1825–1829
Political party: Democratic-Republican
Birthday: July 11, 1767
BEST SWIMMER

WILLIAM H. HARRISON

Old Tippecanoe
Year in office: 1841
Political party: Whig
Birthday: February 9, 1773
MOST LONG-WINDED SPEAKER

JOHN TYLER

His Accidency
Years in office: 1841–1845
Political party: Whig
Birthday: March 29, 1790
MOST LIKELY TO HAVE 15 KIDS

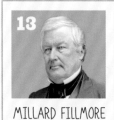

MILLARD FILLMORE

American Louis Philippe
Years in office: 1850–1853
Political party: Whig
Birthday: January 7, 1800
MOST LIKELY TO COMPROMISE

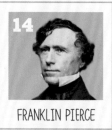

FRANKLIN PIERCE

Young Hickory of the Granite Hills
Years in office: 1853–1857
Political party: Democratic
Birthday: November 23, 1804
HANDSOMEST

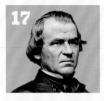

ANDREW JOHNSON

Tennessee Tailor
Years in office: 1865–1869
Political party: Democratic
Birthday: December 29, 1808
THE MOUSE WHISPERER

ULYSSES S. GRANT

Unconditional Surrender
Years in office: 1869–1877
Political party: Republican
Birthday: April 27, 1822
MOST LIKELY TO GET A SPEEDING TICKET

CHESTER A. ARTHUR

Elegant Arthur
Years in office: 1881–1885
Political party: Republican
Birthday: October 5, 1829
BEST DRESSED

GROVER CLEVELAND

Uncle Jumbo
Years in office: 1885–1889
Political party: Democratic
Birthday: March 18, 1837
MOST LIKELY TO BE . . .

THOMAS JEFFERSON

Sage of Monticello
Years in office: 1801–1809
Political party: Democratic-Republican
Birthday: April 13, 1743
BIGGEST BOOKWORM

JAMES MADISON

Father of the Constitution
Years in office: 1809–1817
Political party: Democratic-Republican
Birthday: March 16, 1751
SMALLEST, BUT MIGHTIEST

ANDREW JACKSON

Old Hickory
Years in office: 1829–1837
Political party: Democratic
Birthday: March 15, 1767
MOST LIKELY TO GET IN A DUEL

MARTIN VAN BUREN

Old Kinderhook
Years in office: 1837–1841
Political party: Democratic
Birthday: December 5, 1782
MOST OK

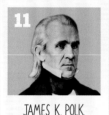

JAMES K. POLK

Young Hickory
Years in office: 1845–1849
Political party: Democratic
Birthday: November 2, 1795
BEST HAIR

ZACHARY TAYLOR

Old Rough and Ready
Years in office: 1849–1850
Political party: Whig
Birthday: November 24, 1784
MOST CASUALLY DRESSED

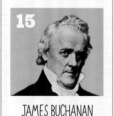

JAMES BUCHANAN

Old Buck
Years in office: 1857–1861
Political party: Democratic
Birthday: April 23, 1791
MOST INDECISIVE

ABRAHAM LINCOLN

Great Emancipator
Years in office: 1861–1865
Political party: Republican
Birthday: February 12, 1809
BEST WRESTLER

RUTHERFORD B. HAYES

Rud
Years in office: 1877–1881
Political party: Republican
Birthday: October 4, 1822
MOST LIKELY TO DRINK LEMONADE

JAMES A. GARFIELD

Preacher President
Year in office: 1881
Political party: Republican
Birthday: November 19, 1831
MOST LIKELY TO SUCCEED

BENJAMIN HARRISON

Human Iceberg
Years in office: 1889–1893
Political party: Republican
Birthday: August 20, 1833
CHILLIEST DEMEANOR

GROVER CLEVELAND

Uncle Jumbo
Years in office: 1893–1897
Political party: Democratic
Birthday: March 18, 1837
. . . SPLIT IN TWO

Idol of Ohio
Years in office: 1897–1901
Political party: Republican
Birthday: January 29, 1843
BEST LAPEL FLOWER

WILLIAM McKINLEY

TR
Years in office: 1901–1909
Political party: Republican
Birthday: October 27, 1858
MOST LIKELY TO EXPLORE THE AMAZON

THEODORE ROOSEVELT

Wobbly Warren
Years in office: 1921–1923
Political party: Republican
Birthday: November 2, 1865
WORST POKER PLAYER

WARREN G. HARDING

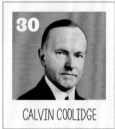

Silent Cal
Years in office: 1923–1929
Political party: Republican
Birthday: July 4, 1872
MOST LIKELY TO TAKE A NAP

CALVIN COOLIDGE

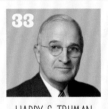

Give 'Em Hell Harry
Years in office: 1945–1953
Political party: Democratic
Birthday: May 8, 1884
BEST SPEED WALKER

HARRY S. TRUMAN

Ike
Years in office: 1953–1961
Political party: Republican
Birthday: October 14, 1890
BEST GOLFER

DWIGHT D. EISENHOWER

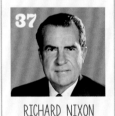

Tricky Dick
Years in office: 1969–1974
Political party: Republican
Birthday: January 9, 1913
BIGGEST BUG LOVER

RICHARD NIXON

Jerry
Years in office: 1974–1977
Political party: Republican
Birthday: July 14, 1913
MOST ATHLETIC

GERALD FORD

Poppy
Years in office: 1989–1993
Political party: Republican
Birthday: June 12, 1924
BEST SKYDIVER

GEORGE H. W. BUSH

Bubba
Years in office: 1993–2001
Political party: Democratic
Birthday: August 19, 1946
BEST SAXOPHONE PLAYER

BILL CLINTON

The Donald
Years in office: 2017–2021
Political party: Republican
Birthday: June 14, 1946
YUUGE

DONALD TRUMP

Amtrak Joe
Years in office: 2021–
Political party: Democratic
Birthday: November 20, 1942
BEST SHADES

JOSEPH R. BIDEN

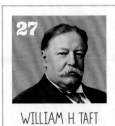

WILLIAM H. TAFT

Big Lub
Years in office: 1909–1913
Political party: Republican
Birthday: September 15, 1857
MOST LIKELY TO BECOME A SUPREME COURT JUSTICE

WOODROW WILSON

Schoolmaster
Years in office: 1913–1921
Political party: Democratic
Birthday: December 28, 1856
MOST LIKELY TO BECOME A PROFESSOR

HERBERT HOOVER

Chief
Years in office: 1929–1933
Political party: Republican
Birthday: August 10, 1874
BEST FISHERMAN

FRANKLIN D. ROOSEVELT

FDR
Years in office: 1933–1945
Political party: Democratic
Birthday: January 30, 1882
BIGGEST STAMP COLLECTOR

JOHN F. KENNEDY

JFK
Years in office: 1961–1963
Political party: Democratic
Birthday: May 29, 1917
MR. POPULAR

LYNDON B. JOHNSON

LBJ
Years in office: 1963–1969
Political party: Democratic
Birthday: August 27, 1908
COOLEST AMPHIBIOUS CAR

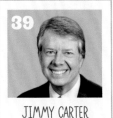

JIMMY CARTER

Hot
Years in office: 1977–1981
Political party: Democratic
Birthday: October 1, 1924
MOST LIKELY TO SEE A UFO

RONALD REAGAN

Dutch
Years in office: 1981–1989
Political party: Republican
Birthday: February 6, 1911
BIGGEST JELLY BEAN LOVER

GEORGE W. BUSH

Dubya
Years in office: 2001–2009
Political party: Republican
Birthday: July 6, 1946
BEST PAINTER

BARACK OBAMA

Barry
Years in office: 2009–2017
Political party: Democratic
Birthday: August 4, 1961
BEST THREE-POINT SHOT

Consider the Source

Power to the People

- CIA World Factbook, cia.gov/the-world-factbook/

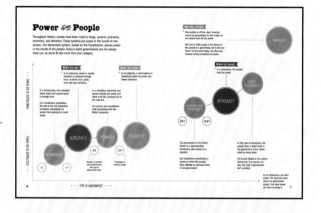

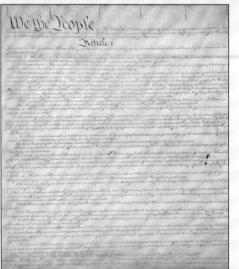

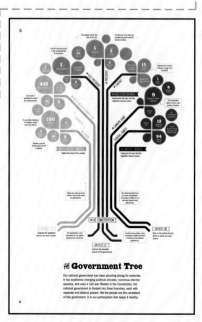

We the People

- Monk, Linda R. *The Words We Live By: Your Annotated Guide to the Constitution.* New York: Hachette Books, 2015.

- National Constitution Center, constitutioncenter.org

- United States Census Bureau, census.gov

- The United States Constitution, archives .gov/founding-docs/constitution-transcript

The first three words of the Constitution were the inspiration for this spread and for much of the content of this book.

The Government Tree

- National Constitution Center, constitutioncenter.org

- United States Courts, uscourts.gov

- The White House, whitehouse.gov

The Periodic Table of the Presidents

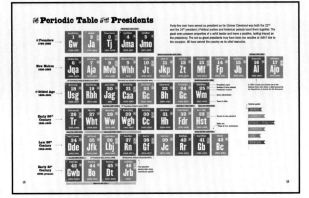

- DeGregorio, William A., and Aaron Jaffe. *The Complete Book of U.S. Presidents*. Fort Lee, NJ: Barricade Books, Inc., 2017.

- Kane, Joseph Nathan, and Janet Podell. *Facts about the Presidents: A Compilation of Biographical and Historical Information*. New York: H.W. Wilson, 2009.

By the Numbers

- Davis, Kenneth C., and Pedro Martin. *Don't Know Much about the Presidents*. New York: HarperCollins Publishers, 2014.

- DeGregorio, William A., and Aaron Jaffe. *The Complete Book of U.S. Presidents*. Fort Lee, NJ: Barricade Books, Inc., 2017.

- History, Art, and Archives: United States House of Representatives, history.house.gov

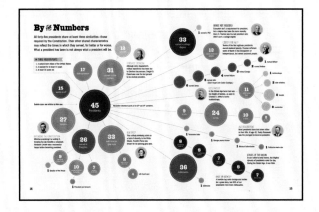

- Kane, Joseph Nathan, and Janet Podell. *Facts about the Presidents: A Compilation of Biographical and Historical Information*. New York: H.W. Wilson, 2009.

- Miller Center, University of Virginia, millercenter.org/the-presidency

- Pastan, Amy. *The Smithsonian Book of Presidential Trivia*. Washington, DC: Smithsonian Books, 2016.

- Thompson, Derek. "The Net Worth of the U.S. Presidents: From Washington to Obama," 2010. theatlantic.com/business/archive/2010/05/the-net-worth-of-the-us-presidents-from-washington-to-obama/57020/.

- United States Senate, senate.gov

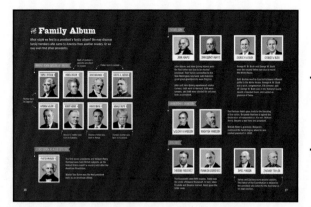

The Family Album

- DeGregorio, William A., and Aaron Jaffe. *The Complete Book of U.S. Presidents*. Fort Lee, NJ: Barricade Books, Inc., 2017.

- Kane, Joseph Nathan, and Janet Podell. *Facts about the Presidents: A Compilation of Biographical and Historical Information*. New York: H.W. Wilson, 2009.

Take Me to Your Leader

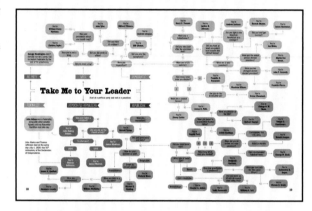

- Davis, Kenneth C., and Pedro Martin. *Don't Know Much about the Presidents*. New York: HarperCollins Publishers, 2014.

- DeGregorio, William A., and Aaron Jaffe. *The Complete Book of U.S. Presidents*. Fort Lee, NJ: Barricade Books, Inc., 2017.

- Kane, Joseph Nathan, and Janet Podell. *Facts about the Presidents: A Compilation of Biographical and Historical Information*. New York: H.W. Wilson, 2009.

- Miller Center, University of Virginia, millercenter.org/the-presidency

- Pastan, Amy. *The Smithsonian Book of Presidential Trivia*. Washington, DC: Smithsonian Books, 2016.

The Political Parties Prism

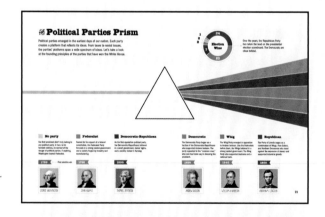

- Maisel, Louis Sandy. *American Political Parties and Elections: A Very Short Introduction*. Oxford: Oxford University Press, 2016.

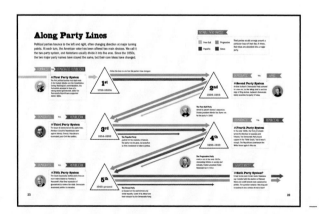

Along Party Lines

- Maisel, Louis Sandy. *American Political Parties and Elections: A Very Short Introduction*. Oxford: Oxford University Press, 2016.

Red State, Blue State

- Electoral College Results, National Archives, archives.gov/electoral-college

- Federal Election Commission, fec.gov

- Smith, Erin Geiger. *Thank You for Voting: The Maddening, Enlightening, Inspiring Truth about Voting in America*. New York: Harper, an imprint of HarperCollins Publishers, 2020.

- Wegman, Jesse. *Let the People Pick the President: The Case for Abolishing the Electoral College*. NY: St. Martin's Press, 2020.

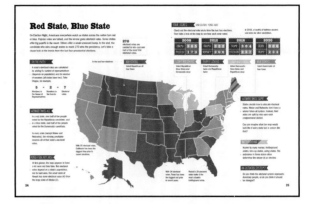

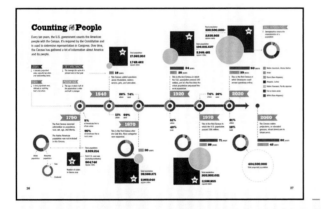

Counting the People

- United States Census Bureau, census.gov. Please note the data for 2020 comes from the 2020 Census, the 2010 Census and the 2019 American Community Survey.

The Issues That Divide Us

- The generalizations presented in this infographic are based on data from the Pew Research Center, pewresearch.org

- Library of Congress, loc.gov

- Smithsonian Institution, si.edu

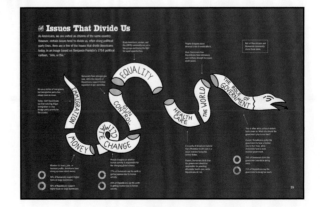

Benjamin Franklin's "Join, or Die" political cartoon, 1754.

Voter Turnout

- The American Presidency Project, University of California Santa Barbara, presidency.ucsb.edu

- Fraga, Bernard L. *The Turnout Gap: Race, Ethnicity, and Political Inequality in a Diversifying America.* Cambridge, United Kingdom: Cambridge University Press, 2019.

- Smith, Erin Geiger. *Thank You for Voting: The Maddening, Enlightening, Inspiring Truth about Voting in America.* New York: Harper, an imprint of HarperCollins Publishers, 2020.

- United States Census Bureau, census.gov

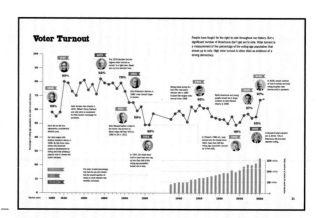

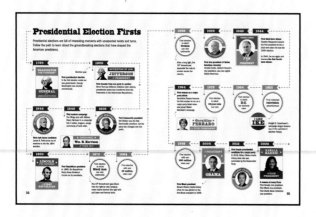

Presidential Election Firsts

- The American Presidency Project, University of California Santa Barbara, presidency.ucsb.edu

- Miller Center, University of Virginia, millercenter.org/the-presidency

Famous First Words

- The American Presidency Project, University of California Santa Barbara, presidency.ucsb.edu

- Encyclopedia Britannica, britannica.com

- Library of Congress, loc.gov

- National Park Service, nps.gov

- United States Senate, senate.gov

- The White House, whitehouse.gov

- The White House Historical Association, whitehousehistory.org

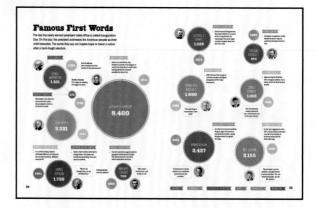

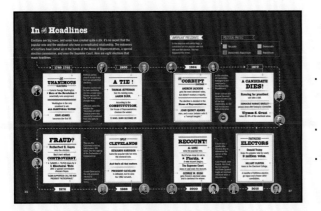

In the Headlines

- Electoral College Results, National Archives, archives.gov/electoral-college

- Encyclopedia Britannica, britannica.com

- Kane, Joseph Nathan, and Janet Podell. *Facts about the Presidents: A Compilation of Biographical and Historical Information*. New York: H.W. Wilson, 2009.

- Maisel, Louis Sandy. *American Political Parties and Elections: A Very Short Introduction*. Oxford: Oxford University Press, 2016.

- Miller Center, University of Virginia, millercenter.org/the-presidency

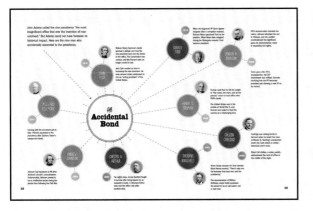

The Accidental Bond

- Cohen, Jared. *Accidental Presidents: Eight Men Who Changed America*. New York: Simon & Schuster Paperbacks, 2020.

- Encyclopedia Britannica, britannica.com

- Harry S. Truman Library and Museum, trumanlibrary.gov

- Kane, Joseph Nathan, and Janet Podell. *Facts about the Presidents: A Compilation of Biographical and Historical Information*. New York: H.W. Wilson, 2009.

- National Portrait Gallery, Smithsonian Institution, npg.si.edu

Lines of Communication

- Library of Congress, loc.gov

- Miller Center, University of Virginia, millercenter.org/the-presidency

- Pew Research Center, pewresearch.org

- Smithsonian Institution, si.edu

- United States Bureau of Labor Statistics, bls.gov

- United States Census Bureau, census.gov

- The White House Historical Association, whitehousehistory.org

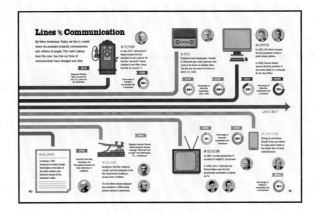

Mail to the Chief

- Barack Obama White House Archives, obamawhitehouse.archives.gov

- Bill Clinton White House Archives, clintonwhitehouse3.archives.gov

- Harry S. Truman Library and Museum, trumanlibrary.gov

- Library of Congress, loc.gov

- Reports of Committees: 16th Congress, 1st Session–49th Congress, 1st Session

- Smith, Ira Robert Taylor, and Joe Alex Morris. *"Dear Mr. President . . ." The Story of Fifty Years in the White House Mail Room*. New York: Julian Messner Inc., 1949.

- The White House, whitehouse.gov

- Young, Dwight. *Dear Mr. President: Letters to the Oval Office from the Files of the National Archives*. Washington, D.C.: National Geographic, 2008.

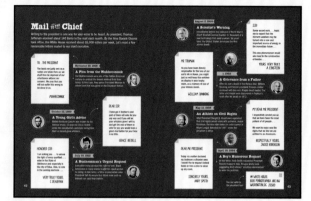

Challenging the President

- Cassidy, Tina. *How Long Must We Wait? Alice Paul, Woodrow Wilson, and the Fight for the Right to Vote*. Atria Books, 2019.

- Library of Congress, loc.gov

- National Park Service, nps.gov

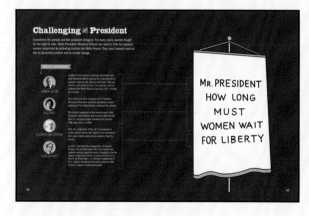

Suffragists picket with banners in front of the White House, 1917.

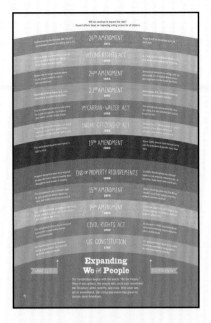

Expanding We the People

- Fraga, Bernard L. *The Turnout Gap: Race, Ethnicity, and Political Inequality in a Diversifying America*. Cambridge, United Kingdom: Cambridge University Press, 2019.

- History, Art, and Archives: United States House of Representatives, history.house.gov

- Keyssar, Alexander. *The Right to Vote: The Contested History of Democracy in the United States*. New York: Basic Books, 2009.

- Library of Congress, loc.gov

- National Constitution Center, constitutioncenter.org

- Smith, Erin Geiger. *Thank You for Voting: The Maddening, Enlightening, Inspiring Truth about Voting in America*. New York: Harper, an imprint of HarperCollins Publishers, 2020.

- United States Census Bureau, census.gov

- United States of America, Department of State, Office of the Historian, history.state.gov

Obstacles to Voting

- Brennan Center for Justice, brennancenter.org

- National Conference of State Legislators, ncsl.org

- Smith, Erin Geiger. *Thank You for Voting: The Maddening, Enlightening, Inspiring Truth about Voting in America*. New York: Harper, an imprint of HarperCollins Publishers, 2020.

- Smithsonian National Museum of American History, americanhistory.si.edu

- United States Census Bureau, census.gov

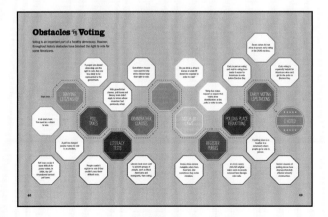

The Gerrymander

- Gerrymander example inspired by FairVote, fairvote.org

- Fraga, Bernard L. *The Turnout Gap: Race, Ethnicity, and Political Inequality in a Diversifying America.* Cambridge, United Kingdom: Cambridge University Press, 2019.

- History, Art, and Archives: United States House of Representatives, history.house.gov

- Library of Congress, loc.gov

- National Conference of State Legislators, ncsl.org

- Smith, Erin Geiger. *Thank You for Voting: The Maddening, Enlightening, Inspiring Truth about Voting in America.* New York: Harper, an imprint of HarperCollins Publishers, 2020.

- Smithsonian National Museum of American History, americanhistory.si.edu

- United States Census Bureau, census.gov

- Please note the districts for California, Ohio, and Texas are based on 2010 apportionment.

The original 1812 broadside ridiculing "The Gerry-mander."

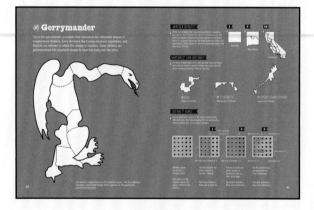

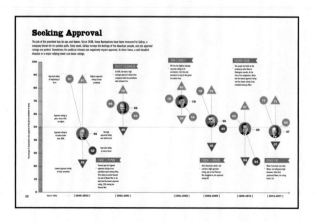

Seeking Approval

- The American Presidency Project, University of California Santa Barbara, presidency.ucsb.edu

- Kane, Joseph Nathan, and Janet Podell. *Facts about the Presidents: A Compilation of Biographical and Historical Information.* New York: H.W. Wilson, 2009.

- Presidential Job Approval Center, Gallup, news.gallup.com/interactives/185273 /presidential-job-approval-center.aspx

The Next Chapter

- Miller Center, University of Virginia, millercenter.org/the-presidency

- National Archives Presidential Libraries and Museums, archives.gov/presidential-libraries

- Updegrove, Mark K. *Second Acts: Presidential Lives and Legacies after the White House.* Guilford, CT: Lyons Press, 2018.

We Can Do It!

- The American Presidency Project, University of California Santa Barbara, presidency.ucsb.edu

- Cesar Chavez Foundation, chavezfoundation.org

- Edward M. Kennedy Institute for the United States Senate, emkinstitute.org

- Library of Congress, loc.gov

- National Archives Presidential Libraries and Museums, archives.gov/presidential-libraries

- National Constitution Center, constitutioncenter.org

- National Park Service, nps.gov

- National Women's History Museum, womenshistory.org

- Radcliffe Institute for Advanced Study, Harvard University, radcliffe.harvard.edu

- Smithsonian National Museum of American History, americanhistory.si.edu

- Teaching American History, teachingamericanhistory.org

- Twain, Mark. *The Gilded Age and Later Novels.* New York: The Library of America, 2007.

- University of Virginia School of Law, law.virginia.edu

This popular World War II poster introduced Rosie the Riveter as an icon of American determination.

A Lasting Memory

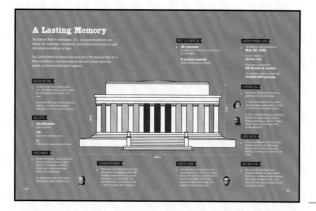

- A Guide to the Lincoln Memorial, District of Columbia, National Park Service Division of Publications, 1986.

- National Park Service, nps.gov

The Presidential Yearbook

- DeGregorio, William A., and Stuart, S. L. *The Complete Book of U.S. Presidents; with updates by Sandra Lee Stuart.* Fort Lee, NJ: Barricade, 2009.

- Kane, Joseph Nathan, and Janet Podell. *Facts about the Presidents: A Compilation of Biographical and Historical Information.* New York: H.W. Wilson, 2009.

- O'Brien, Cormac. *Secret Lives of the U.S. Presidents: What Your Teachers Never Told You about the Men of the White House.* United States: Hallmark Gift Books, Quirk Books, 2012.

- Periodic Presidents, periodicpresidents.com

- Rubel, David. *Scholastic Encyclopedia of the Presidents and Their Times.* New York: Scholastic, 2013.

A Note of Thanks

We are grateful to Macmillan and Roaring Brook Press for giving us this opportunity. Thank you to everyone who had a hand in bringing this book to life. In particular, we would like to thank Emily Feinberg, Jennifer Healey, Mike Burroughs, Sharismar Rodriguez, Sherri Schmidt, Janet Renard, and Susan Bishansky for their brilliance, guidance, and expertise. Thank you, Josalyn Moran, for your faith in us. And to our family, for your unending support.

Image Sources

The authors gratefully acknowledge the following sources for the images in this book:

Clinton White House Archives: Al Gore; **History, Art & Archives / U.S. House of Representatives:** Geraldine Ferraro, John Lewis; **Library of Congress:** Thomas Jefferson, John Tyler, James Polk, Zachary Taylor, James Buchanan, Abraham Lincoln, Rutherford Hayes, James Garfield, Chester Arthur, William McKinley, Theodore Roosevelt, Warren Harding, Calvin Coolidge, Herbert Hoover, Franklin Roosevelt, Dwight Eisenhower, John Kennedy, Lyndon Johnson, Gerald Ford, Jimmy Carter, Ronald Reagan, George H. W. Bush, Bill Clinton, George W. Bush, Barack Obama, Donald Trump, Joseph R. Biden, Lucretia Mott, Elizabeth Cady Stanton, Alice Paul, Charles Curtis, Aaron Burr, Horace Greeley, Samuel Tilden, Albert Einstein, Marian Anderson, Frederick Douglass, Mark Twain, Susan B. Anthony, Shirley Chisholm, Thurgood Marshall, "Join, or Die" cartoon, 1917 picketing suffragists image, "The Gerry-Mander" broadside; **National Archives:** Richard Nixon, Jackie Robinson, Martin Luther King, Constitution image, "We Can Do It!" poster; **National Gallery of Art**: Andrew Jackson; **National Portrait Gallery:** George Washington, John Adams, James Madison, James Monroe, John Q. Adams, Martin Van Buren, William Harrison, Millard Fillmore, Franklin Pierce, Andrew Johnson, Ulysses Grant, Grover Cleveland, Benjamin Harrison, William Taft, Woodrow Wilson, Harry Truman, Benjamin Franklin, Alexander Hamilton; **Supreme Court of the U.S.:** Ruth Bader Ginsburg; **U.S. Department of State:** Hillary Clinton; **U.S. Senate:** Kamala Harris; **Wikimedia Commons:** Grace Bedell.